Encountering
the Sacred

T0353236

Encountering the Sacred

Feminist Reflections on Women's Lives

Edited by
Rebecca Todd Peters
and Grace Y. Kao

t&tclark

LONDON • NEW YORK • OXFORD • NEW DELHI • SYDNEY

T&T CLARK
Bloomsbury Publishing Plc
50 Bedford Square, London, WC1B 3DP, UK
1385 Broadway, New York, NY 10018, USA

BLOOMSBURY, T&T CLARK and the T&T Clark logo are trademarks
of Bloomsbury Publishing Plc

First published in Great Britain 2019

Copyright © Rebecca Todd Peters, Grace Y. Kao and contributors, 2019

Rebecca Todd Peters and Grace Y. Kao have asserted their right under
the Copyright, Designs and Patents Act, 1988, to be identified as
Editors of this work.

Unless otherwise indicated, all Scripture quotations are from the New
Revised Standard Version of the Bible (NRSV), copyright © 1989 National
Council of the Churches of Christ in the United States of America. Used by
permission. All rights reserved.

For legal purposes the Acknowledgments on p. ix constitute an extension
of this copyright page.

Cover image: Title: Sophia and Her Sisters; Artist: Nalini Jayasuriya;
Photograph Credit: Natalie Carter Hyde/Aesthetic Images Photography, Inc.

All rights reserved. No part of this publication may be reproduced or transmitted
in any form or by any means, electronic or mechanical, including photocopying,
recording, or any information storage or retrieval system, without prior
permission in writing from the publishers.

Bloomsbury Publishing Plc does not have any control over, or responsibility for,
any third-party websites referred to or in this book. All internet addresses given
in this book were correct at the time of going to press. The author and publisher
regret any inconvenience caused if addresses have changed or sites have ceased
to exist, but can accept no responsibility for any such changes.

A catalogue record for this book is available from the British Library.

A catalog record for this book is available from the Library of Congress.

ISBN: HB: 978-0-5676-8301-4
PB: 978-0-5676-8300-7
ePDF: 978-0-5676-8303-8
ePUB: 978-0-5676-8302-1

Typeset by Deanta Global Publishing Services, Chennai, India

To find out more about our authors and books visit www.bloomsbury.com
and sign up for our newsletters.

We dedicate this book to future generations
of feminist theologians

CONTENTS

ACKNOWLEDGMENTS

This book is a culmination of a vision—hashed out over countless conversations and late nights at the American Academy of Religion (AAR) and the Society of Christian Ethics (SCE)—to do feminist theology in a new way. More than fifty feminist scholars of religion responded affirmatively to an email inquiry way back in November 2011 to discuss a new project intending to make feminist theologies more accessible to lay or nontheologically trained women. Dozens of women participated in those early discussions, offering insight and practical suggestions. We thank all those many colleagues and friends who have helped to shape this vision with us. Indeed, many more than the twelve women represented in this volume offered ideas and abstracts for chapters they would like to write, and we hope to eventually find ways to bring their voices to broader publics.

We especially thank the women who offered up their talents, perspectives, and personal experiences as contributors to *Encountering the Sacred*. We thank Elon University and Claremont School of Theology for financially sponsoring our two writing retreats (New York and California), where all book contributors assembled—over good food and drink as well as laughter and tears—to sharpen the project's focus and workshop our chapters. Thanks also to Sarah Holland who helped with logistical arrangements for our first retreat. We also bear a debt of gratitude to those who gave us helpful advice at various points in our long journey to publication: Susan Reed, Sarah Sentilles, Elizabeth Wales, William Critzman, Kwok Pui-lan, and Nancy Fitzgerald. Finally, special thanks to Anna Turton and Sarah Blake from Bloomsbury Press who recognized the importance and value of our vision and have supported us through the process of moving this project to publication.

Introduction:

Feminist theology as conversation and invitation

Rebecca Todd Peters
and Grace Y. Kao

On June 28, 2018, more than 500 women staged a sit-in against family separation and detention at the US Senate's Hart Office Building. At issue was the Trump administration's "zero tolerance" policy against anyone caught entering the United States outside of officially designated ports of entry—including asylum-seekers. These protesters were cleverly draped in foil blankets to evoke those painful images of migrant children without their parents, and in some cases in barbed-wire cages, for having crossed the border "illegally." They were also dressed in white, so as to visually unify the crowd and harken back to powerful and iconic movements for social change, including for women's suffrage. At least four women senators joined them, including Tammy Duckworth (D-IL) with her eleven-week-old daughter wrapped snugly to her chest—the first senator to have given birth while in office. Various news outlets report that these hundreds of immigration-policy protesters were subsequently arrested for civil disobedience.

Feminists do not always wear white and chant "Abolish ICE" (Immigration and Customs Enforcement) when they stand up for justice. Sometimes they wear pink "pussy" hats, as hundreds of thousands did on January 21, 2017, during the Women's March (in Washington, DC, and elsewhere, including outside of the United States) to protest the presidential inauguration of Donald Trump one day earlier. Sometimes they chant "hands up, don't shoot" while raising their hands accordingly to protest police brutality as per the "black lives matter" movement founded by three black women in 2013. And sometimes women old enough to be grandmothers campaign for various peace and environmental causes by playfully wearing clothes associated with older women and singing their political messages to the tune of well-known songs as the "raging grannies" do across the United States and Canada.

Though disparate, what unites these women-led movements is the feminist commitment to embodied activism and social change. We follow bell hooks's insight that feminism "simply put . . . is a movement to end sexism, sexist exploitation, and oppression."[1] While this position begins with the fundamental assumption of women's and men's equality, it goes far beyond a common liberal, white feminist emphasis on rights. Intersectional feminism requires recognizing the ways in which various forms of prejudice and bias or intolerance work together to create social, political, and economic structures of oppression. However, being a feminist requires more than an intellectual acknowledgment of these realities: it requires an individual to act.

Choosing to be a feminist is a political and spiritual decision that must be made in the full knowledge of the forces one is up against. Those who claim to support equality and to reject exploitation but refuse the label "feminist" and the requisite work are often afraid of making waves or challenging the status quo—even if they do not agree with it. But, as feminist social ethicist Beverly Harrison reminded us, anger (e.g., against injustice) is not always negative and confrontation is often necessary in the process of social change.[2] It is thus often people willing to stand up and speak out against injustice who have no compunctions about claiming a feminist identity. Thus, to the extent that feminists are those who are reasonably demanding—and agitating for—the structures and institutions of our world (government, the law, schools, religious organizations, our jobs, etc.) to reflect the socially accepted fact that men and women not only *are* equal, but also *ought to be treated* so, feminism is for everybody willing to do the work.

To be a Christian feminist is to have one's feminism infused with the radical justice-love that reflects the best part of the Christian tradition and to embody a religious faith that expresses an unwavering commitment to the inclusion and care of the world's most marginalized people and other parts of creation. It is to recognize and name the patriarchy and misogyny that is embedded in the Christian tradition while actively seeking the life-giving power of the sacred that has also always been present in it as well. In these pages, we invite you to learn about feminist theology and to draw on the insights of feminist Christian scholars as we share our encounters with the sacred and collectively search for the ways in which our lives and our theologies are part of the larger task of seeking justice and peace in the world.

Origins of feminist theologies

Feminist theology was born in the 1960s as part of a larger movement known as "liberation theology" that broke open traditionalist, hierarchical approaches to faith, spirituality, and humanity's relationship with God. Liberation theologies affirmed the practical wisdom and knowledge of God that grows out of people's lived experiences.

It also opened the door to rereading the Bible and rethinking the Christian tradition from the perspective of women; the poor; sexual minorities; nonwhite, non-Western, or postcolonial subjects; and still others living on the margins of society, of Christianity, or of other kinds of power in our world. Liberation theologies recognized that people on the edges of society are often able to see things about the dominant culture that are either invisible to or ignored by those who hold power and status in society. This was originally referred to as "the epistemological privilege of the poor," which means that the poor often have a better vantage point from which to grasp the structural problems in society that contribute to economic inequality and policies that contribute to the impoverishment of the poor.

The women who first began to do theology as feminists recognized that women's daily lives and everyday experiences gave women power and insight to glimpse the sacred in ways that not only differed from the male theologians who had shaped Christian doctrine for centuries, but allowed them to apprehend what their powerful male counterparts could not. Similar to the "epistemological privilege of the poor," this is a key insight of what is called "feminist standpoint theory"—that where people "stand" in society shapes what and how they behold and experience the world. A second key insight is that, because the dominant ideas in society have largely been shaped by those with more status and power, people on the underside or margins of power who have a different vantage point are able to see where conventional wisdom fails.[3] In matters of religion or theology, feminists have shown how women's ways of being in the world have allowed them to view issues like sin and justice, relationship and divinity, differently and in some cases, superiorly.

In 1960, Valerie Saiving made this abundantly evident when she famously challenged the then-dominant Christian teaching that "man's" greatest sin was pride. In observing that women of her era were more likely to undervalue themselves than unduly puff themselves up, she demonstrated how dominant Christian theology not only reflected male experience but also assumed that men's particular experience reflected universal human reality. Saiving argued instead that since many women were prone to discount or negate themselves as a result of their gender socialization under patriarchy, the traditional Christian encouragement toward the virtue of "selflessness" (as an antidote to pride) would likely do them more harm than good.[4]

To be sure, as white women began to develop new visions of feminist theology, women of color, women from the global South, lesbian or queer women, women with disabilities, and others were quick to point out the limitations of those liberative perspectives that essentialized sex or universalized gender ("all women are the same and face the same struggles") and thereby failed to recognize the complexity of—and variation in—women's experiences. Consider, for example, what famed (black) poet and theorist Audre Lorde cautioned white women in an address at Amherst College in 1980: "Some problems we share as women, some we do not. You fear your children will grow up to join the patriarchy and testify against you; we fear our children will be dragged from a car and shot down in the street, and you will turn your backs upon the reasons they are dying."[5] That Lorde's words predated the "Black Lives Matter" movement by more than thirty years underscores how vast the differences between many black and white women's experiences have been and continue to be.

Not surprisingly, these differences have made their way into black women's contributions to the development of feminist theologies. In 1986, Delores S. Williams recounted a story about the response of a black churchwoman to a lecture she had given on feminist theology.

> Honey [addressing Williams], I want to say something about this feminism if you can bear with me. [I nodded my head indicating that I could.] This all reminds me of the day I went into a fancy dress shop downtown and saw a real pretty dress. The colors in the dress blended right. The design was modern and fashionable. The buttons in front looked real pretty with the material. Everything about that dress looked just right. There was only one problem when it came right down to it. The dress was size five, and I wear size twenty. The saleslady told me that shop didn't carry no dresses over size thirteen. I can sew real good, but I knew there was no way for me to alter that dress and still have the same thing. There just wasn't enough material in that dress to make it fit me. Now that's point, honey. This feminism looks real pretty, but there just ain't enough in it to fit me. And what I'm wondering is: if you black feminists try to make feminism fit me, will you have the same thing?[6]

As Williams and other black women theologians began to develop their own theological voices, they drew upon Pulitzer Prize–winning Alice Walker's work to develop "womanism" as a specific form of liberation theological discourse reflecting the lived experiences of many black women and the theological burdens and insights that emerged from them.[7] Today, theology by both self-identified black feminists and womanists continues to flourish, as does the scholarship and activism from other feminists of color and feminists from the global South (viz., *mujeristas* and Latina feminists, Asian and Asian American feminists, Native and indigenous feminists).[8]

In short, these and many other internal critics have been advocating for not only the power of self-naming, but also an "intersectional" approach to social analysis.[9] They have been pointing out to their white colleagues that experiences of oppression are not additive—they do not simply stack up on top of each other (i.e., "I am oppressed in this way because I am *Asian*, this way because I am a *woman*, and this way because I am *bisexual*"). Rather, the oppression minoritized communities encounter has been specific to the ways in which their identities intersect or combine to shape their social reality. After all, people don't interact with the various aspects of an individual's identity separately. There is not one reaction to a person's race that is separate from the response to that person's gender expression or perceived abilities or sexual orientation. When people interact with others, they react to the whole person in front of them with all the assumptions and prejudices they hold. This is evident from the fact that poor black women are treated differently from disabled white lesbians who are themselves often treated differently from Latina professionals or mixed-race trans women activists and so forth.[10] Women who experience multiple forms of oppression have named the colonialism, racism, and other essentialist assumptions in large swaths of liberal white feminist thought and have sought to make visible the complexity of their marginalization and their experiences of white supremacist patriarchy and Western hegemony.

These mistakes and omissions should not be minimized. Taken as a whole, however, what even the earliest feminist and other liberation theologies did is not only transgress the *boundaries* of traditional theology, but also break open its *task* in ways that invited the experiences, insights, and gifts of successive generations of the less powerful to serve as the foundation for knowing and experiencing the divine.[11] By reflecting on their different social locations and lived experiences, feminists of all stripes and other liberationists have added to the richness of our collective theological inquiries about God and our place in the world amid all of creation. They have done so by asking new questions and answering age-old ones (e.g., about the human condition and our purpose in the world) in new and different ways—ways that have challenged and even threatened the power structures of both the sociopolitical status quo and traditional Christianity. Over the decades, as women from many different spaces, places, contexts, cultures, and life experiences have contributed to building feminist theologies, we have woven a new fabric together—a fabric that reflects the diversity of peoples around the world.

Embracing feminist theology as social change

Much of the early feminist struggle was focused on getting a seat at the (proverbial) table. We think back on some of our feminist foremothers who felt pressured to mimic men when they slipped through the patriarchal door: dressing in suits or clerical robes that were designed for men, teaching and preaching in traditionally masculine ways, and adapting themselves to the hierarchically identified liturgies, structures, and theologies in order to facilitate their access to the patriarchal structures that had only begrudgingly admitted them.

Of course, the idea that feminism is only or primarily about equality between the sexes has its roots in both the first and the second waves of feminism, where activists were pushing for women's suffrage, the rights of girls/women to the same educational and work opportunities as boys/men, and other reforms. Today, however, many feminists are advocating for far more than mere formal equality between the sexes. They are also seeking to empower women to live flourishing and fulfilling lives—a task that often requires significant attention to building girls'/women's self-esteem and sense of possibilities as well as challenging religious and social norms on the cultural-symbolic level that continue to instruct women to "stay in their place." Because of intersectionality and the interlocking nature of oppression, they are also seeking the liberation of *all* marginalized peoples and the rest of creation (i.e., nonhuman nature) through the transformation of social structures that have been used for harm and injury. Finally, they are refusing to accept that patriarchal, or what Elisabeth Schüssler Fiorenza has called "kyriarchal,"[12] power that demands submission and obedience from the most vulnerable is the only way to shape or structure power in our lives, churches, or world. Letty Russell expressed this idea in her pivotal text *Church in the Round*:

> In feminist styles of leadership, authority is exercised by standing with others by seeking to share power and authority. Power is seen as something to be multiplied and shared rather than accumulated at the top. A feminist leader is one who inspires others to be leaders.[13]

Indeed, a great example of feminist power-sharing is the Pacific, Asian, and North American Asian Women in Theology and Ministry (PANAAWTM)—a network and annual conference founded by the pioneering likes of Kwok Pui-lan and Rita Nakashima Brock in the mid-1980s with assistance from Russell.[14] PANAAWTM continues today to operate on a volunteer basis with decentralized leadership (i.e., no executives, only a steering committee) and with those with the most institutional power and resources (i.e., senior and mid-career professors, pastors of congregations or others with denominational connections and influence) fundraising year-round to be able to host annual conferences at low cost to participants as well as provide significant scholarships for students to attend.[15]

The DNA of feminism and feminist theology, in sum, is its pursuit of social change and its making way for new structures and new modes of being. When we examine the history of theological ideas we can see that Christian understanding and interpretation of various theological concepts and doctrines have shifted and changed over time. Few Christians today hold the same beliefs that marked the early church, nor do we worship in exactly the same way. Yes, there are traditions we have inherited—baptism, communion, ordination—but our understanding of these traditions has also changed and evolved over time. This is what it means to be part of a *living* faith tradition. Feminist theologies are rooted in a commitment to the transformation of patriarchal religious beliefs and practices that mistreat women, other disenfranchised peoples, and the earth. Feminist theological reflection can also be thought of as an expression of contextual theology in its recognition that theology is always developed in response to the particular social, historical, and cultural contexts in which people live.

Even as liberation approaches have radically transformed theological discourse, feminist theologies have often remained hidden from ordinary Christians and the public-at-large in the ivory towers of the academy. Too often the insights of feminist theologians have been stuck in classrooms, disseminated only in specialized conferences, lost in obscure journals, or buried in libraries. While some people might be exposed to these ideas in college or seminary, most Christians have had little or no direct access to the insights and contributions feminist theologies have offered to Christian thought and practice over the past half century. Even though the feminist movement has transformed our culture and our world, the transformative power that feminist theology offers for enriching and expanding people's theological reflection and their encounter with the divine has all too often eluded many ordinary people. As Christian women who are also feminist scholars of religion and active in our churches and other social justice or healing ministries, we wrote this book to invite women of faith into new spaces where we could think together about our lives as women shaping our faith and our faith helping to make sense of our lives. We are feminists, womanists, and *mujeristas* who largely did not have to break down the door (to get inside the church,[16] academy, or board room as our foremothers did), and thus could move beyond basic (sexist) questions about our equality or our right to be there.[17] We have had the luxury to strategize about how we would like to rearrange the furniture in what the popular musical Hamilton sings of the "room where it happens" now that we are here. When finding that the rigidity and discomfort of centuries-old rectangular tables, throne-like chairs, and "ivory towers" does not suit our bodies' needs, we have worked to change them. We have been led by the inclusive spirit of our hearts that seeks to draw all God's children to the round table of fellowship where we can meet as equals. And we have, in the midst of our notable differences, recognized powerful sources of knowledge in the lived experience of women and others who have been denied access to the structures of power in church and society.

An overview of the book and invitation to readers

What follows are ten chapters by ten remarkable women, all of whom have doctorates in religion or theology and are engaged in the feminist theological enterprise in their capacities as professors, activists, ministers, and scholars. As a group, we are reformers and revolutionaries, Catholic and Protestant, lay and clergy, queer and straight, single and married, parents and without children, white and of color. As we share deeply personal aspects of our embodied existence and reflect theologically about them, we invite you to do the same by allowing our feminist insights about our lives and the sacred to serve as windows into your own.

You will find in the subsequent chapters both an embrace of and a wrestling with Christianity as a living faith tradition. As a group, we find sources of inspiration from the teachings and theologies we have inherited, like María Teresa Dávila does with the Gospel stories of solidarity with the poor in her reflections on living simply or like Kendra G. Hotz does in her use of Calvin's notion of vocation for an unconventional end—to explain her certainty that she has not been "called" to parenthood. And we also interrogate, challenge, and subvert the Christianities of our youth, as both Marcia Mount Shoop and Monica A. Coleman do when they question the value of redemptive suffering in the atonement in their experiences of rape and miscarriage, respectively. We mine the Bible for wisdom and the stories of women in particular, as Gina Messina does when she shares in Sarah's desperation, Rachel's envy, and Hannah's hope in her years-long struggle with infertility, or as Victoria Rue does when reading Psalm 23 to her terminally ill mother helps her mother to die in peace and Victoria to meditate on the role of fear in death and dying in her work as a hospice chaplain. And we also creatively fill in the blanks when important details are missing or lost from Scripture, as Kate Ott does when she champions the sacral power of women's friendships by imagining what kind of relationships Jephthah's daughter cultivated with others both before and after her execution by her father in the book of Judges. We participate in traditional Christian rituals or practices for comfort, as Ellen Ott Marshall beautifully does when the Eucharist serves as a source of healing for her while on pregnancy-related bed rest. And we also either seek to reclaim "lost" Christian traditions, such as when Elizabeth Hinson-Hasty retrieves the medieval practices of "God-sibs" and "churching" when making a case for the constructive value of gossip, or we innovate liturgically, as Grace Ji-Sun Kim does by ending her reflections on the racism she and her daughter have endured with a litany for the church to become a beacon of hope and inclusivity.

We make no claim here to be "representing" all women, nor are we suggesting that the powerful experiences our contributors have recounted are the most important ones for women or for feminist theology now. We recognize that any collection, including ours, can only include a slice of myriad women's experiences. In divulging meaningful and significant aspects of their lives, our authors are engaging in the sometimes difficult and sometimes joyful work of theologizing in a feminist key about them. It is our hope that readers will be moved by their stories, inspired by their vulnerability, challenged by their feminist theological insights, and welcomed to reflect on aspects of their own lives in feminist theological ways as well.

We invite you to explore this volume with us. There is no "right" way to read this book, meaning that the remaining chapters need not be read in the order in which they are presented. We do hope that this book will serve as an impetus for dialogue and exchange. To connect feminist theory to practice, we conclude each chapter with a ritual, prayer or blessing, order of service, or some other call to action. To help spark conversations in classrooms, churches, or book clubs, we offer discussion questions at the end of each chapter. Finally, to assist those readers eager to learn more about feminist theology, we list several suggestions for further reading at each chapter's close.

Conclusion

Feminist theologies offer the possibility of the creation of a church and a faith transformed by the radical mutuality and justice inherent in following the wisdom and justice traditions of Christianity. Feminist theologies help us not just to imagine but also to build more just and inclusive churches and broader societies. In a world of sexual and economic exploitation, racism, violence, and misogyny, each of us must daily choose to be feminist and to continue to struggle for justice. When we become weary, we must lean on one another and on God for our support in that struggle. Lean with us now, into her presence, into the presence of the divine as we move forward into new possibilities for encountering the sacred in our lives and in our times.

Notes

1 bell hooks, *Feminism is For Everybody: Passionate Politics*, 2nd edition (New York: Routledge, 2014), 1.

2 Beverly Wildung Harrison, "The Power of Anger in the Work of Love," *Making the Connections: Essays in Feminist Social Ethics*, Boston: Beacon, 1985.

3 For more on "feminist standpoint theory," see especially the chapters by Sandra Harding and Nancy C. M. Hartsock in *The Feminist Standpoint Theory Reader: Intellectual and Political Controversies,* edited by Sandra Harding (New York: Routledge, 2004).

4 Valerie Saiving Goldstein, "The Human Situation: A Feminine View," *Journal of Religion* 40.2 (1960): 100–12.

5 Audre Lorde, *Sister Outsider: Essays and Speeches,* reprint edition (Crossing Press, 2007 [1984]), 119.

6 Delores S. Williams, "The Color of Feminism: Or Speaking the Black Woman's Tongue," *Journal of Religious Thought* 43 (1986).

7 See Alice Walker's four-pronged definition of "womanist" in her *In Search of Our Mothers' Gardens: Womanist Prose* (New York: Harcourt, 1983).

8 For an insightful discussion of the areas of overlap and differences between black feminism and womanism, see Monica A. Coleman et al., "Roundtable Discussion: Must I Be a Womanist?" *Journal of Feminist Studies in Religion* 22.1 (2006): 85–134 and Traci C. West, "Is a Womanist a Black Feminist? Marking the Distinctions and Defying Them: A Black Feminist Response," in *Deeper Shades of Purple: Womanism in Religion and Society,* edited by Stacey M. Floyd-Thomas (New York: New York University Press, 2006), 292–95.

9 Black legal scholar Kimberlé Crenshaw originally coined the term "intersectionality" in her "Demarginalizing the Intersection of Race and Sex: A Black Feminist Critique of Antidiscrimination Doctrine, Feminist Theory, and Antiracist Politics," *University of Chicago Legal Forum* (1989): 139–67.

10 Of course, if their various intersectional identities were not immediately visible or known, they were usually treated stereotypically based on people's understanding of the norm or perceptions about their identities.

11 This is not to imply that the traditional theology of white male theologians is "universal" while the theologies emerging from those who specifically name and theorize from their social location are "particular" with limited application, for we have come to see that *all* theology is "contextual," including theology that is not explicitly named as such, for it emerges from a particular place and time.

12 Elisabeth Schüssler Fiorenza, *Wisdom Ways: Introducing Feminist Biblical Interpretation* (New York: Orbis Books, 2001).

13 Letty Russell, *Church in the Round: Feminist Interpretation of the Church* (Louisville, KY: Westminster John Knox Press, 1993), 57.

14 Several of the thirteen Asian and Asian North American women who first met together in 1984 belonged to an association of women in ministry organized in 1978 in Berkeley, California, through the Pacific Asian Center for Theology and Strategies (PACTS) at the Pacific School of Religion. We thank Rita Nakashima Brock for this oral history.

15 See http://www.panaawtm.org/about/ for more information about PANAAWTM.

16 One exception to this is one of our contributors, Victoria Rue, whose ordination as a priest is not officially recognized by the Catholic Church given its dogmatic insistence on an all-male priesthood.

17 In the midst of the #metoo movement spearheaded by Tarana Burke, we lament the sexual harassment and violence that was par for the course in their generation, and we thank our foremothers for their vulnerability in sharing their stories and mentoring successive generations of women who have had to deal with similar threats, abuses, and trauma.

Questions for discussion

1 This chapter begins with questions about the meaning of feminism. How do you understand the term? Is there a minimal requirement for someone to be a feminist (e.g., must one have embodied experiences as a woman, such that men can only be feminist allies but not feminists proper)? Is feminism primarily about achieving nondiscrimination on the basis of sex or gender, or is feminism advocating for something far more expansive as the authors suggest?

2 A hallmark of feminist or liberative approaches to theology is that it takes seriously the starting point of reflection—a person or people's lived experiences and social location. What do you take to be the advantages and potential disadvantages of explicitly naming one's social context in one's theologizing?

3 Rebecca Todd and Grace summarize the ways in which successive generations of feminist scholarship have been more attentive to differences among women along the lines of race, class, sexual orientation, and so forth. In your judgment, have these "course corrections" mostly served the larger feminist movement well? Or do you fear that "too much" attention to the differences between and among women may splinter the movement to end sexist oppression and shortchange the sources of solidarity and support that can be found?

4 This introduction concludes with very short descriptions of the topics and personal experiences the contributors will take up in successive chapters. Is there a particular one you are looking forward to reading? Why? If you were going to write about your life, what experience would you lift up?

Suggestions for further reading

Chung, Hyun Kyung. *Struggle To Be the Sun Again: Introducing Asian Women's Theology.* New York: Orbis, 1990.
Daly, Mary. *Beyond God the Father: Toward a Philosophy of Women's Liberation.* Boston: Beacon Press, 1973.

Harrison, Beverly Wildung, and Carol S. Robb. *Making the Connections: Essays in Feminist Social Ethics*. Boston: Beacon Press, 1985.

Isasi-Diaz, Ada Maria. *Mujerista Theology: A Theology for the 21st Century*. New York: Orbis Books, 1996.

Kwok, Pui-lan. *Postcolonial Imagination and Feminist Theology*. Louisville, KY: Westminster John Knox Press, 2005.

Oduyoye, Mercy Amba. *Daughters of Anowa: African Women and Patriarchy*. New York: Orbis Books, 1995.

Ruether, Rosemary Radford. *Sexism and God Talk: Toward a Feminist Theology*. Boston: Beacon Press, 1983.

Williams, Delores S. *Sisters in the Wilderness: The Challenge of Womanist God-Talk*. Maryknoll, NY: Orbis Books, 1993.

1

Why we need besties *(friendship)*[1]

Kate Ott

On the bulletin board in my home, next to my kids' practice schedules, the school lunch calendar, church council meeting dates, and long passed invitations, hangs a postcard with these words: "To have a friend is to invite someone closer and closer to the sacred chamber of the heart. To be a friend is to tread softly there." Like many of the items on the bulletin board, this postcard had faded into a mosaic of to-do's or not-done's with no particular uniqueness to any one piece. But, one day, as I was trying to write new words about friendship and faith, I saw the postcard in a new light. I had been thinking about the sacred aspects of friendship and how important it is to create sacred spaces, or sacred chambers, where friendships can flourish. In our daily living, it's easy to lose sight of the sacredness of friendship.

I believe that women's friendships in particular can create a sacred space and become an example of God's radical love in our world. As women, we are reminded daily that we are not good enough as we are. In subtle and not-so-subtle ways, we are made to understand that we need makeup, diets, and new clothes to be pretty; relationships with men and children to validate us; and ladylike manners to play our socially appropriate roles in society. Women's friendships occupy a strange space because they are often defined in reference to men or a male norm. Nevertheless, they hold the potential of being the space where we women love each other into being who God created us to be and where we support one another as we push against these negative cultural messages about who and what we are supposed to be and do. Many of us may find it difficult to uncover the image of God within ourselves under the many layers of social expectations and patriarchal religious imagery. This is a unique challenge. As we love each other, support each other, listen to each other, and create spaces where we can open ourselves to one another without fear of shame or judgment, we show each other "who God is" in an image we rarely see—God as female. Thus, women's friendships can become *sacred* spaces where we reveal God to each another.

Jephthah's daughter: A story of women's friendship

The scriptures do not provide very many examples of women's friendship. Those that do—Rachel and Leah, Ruth and Naomi, Mary and Martha—have to be filled in by imaginative connections because the text itself does not always offer the full story. The book *The Red Tent* by Anita Diamant is a wonderful example of this kind of theological imagination that retells the tale of the sisters Rachel and Leah who became the wives of Jacob (Gen. 29–35). Given the paucity of detail about women's lives in the Bible, the author imagines with us the story of women's private lives that are lost to the biblical record.

Through Diamant's narrative voice, the competition of Jacob's wives is transformed into Dinah's story (Leah's daughter) where we learn how women's relationships became opportunities for them to find sacred space, even as their lives were still largely defined in reference to men and male norms. Women joined together in the Red Tent when they were menstruating, a gathering based solely on their biology as women. While their space apart was tinged with concerns about religious impurity, there was also tremendous power in the space they created outside of men's knowledge and control. The Red Tent empowered women as they nurtured one another through ancient practices of midwifery. The safety of this space not only allowed for the sharing of secrets,[2] but also the humanization of one another in ways not allowed in the world of men that existed beyond the tent's shroud. Outside the tent, women were only seen for their social value to the males in the family: mother, food provider, sexual partner, and so on, thus causing competition among the women. Within the Red Tent, the women created a sacred space where they were full, multidimensional persons who shared their spirituality, social struggles, and familial commitment with all members, including the education of the girl children.

The book of Judges in the Bible hints at another tale of women's friendship, albeit with less detail even than that of Rachel and Leah. In this story, Jephthah, desperate to win a military battle, vows to God that he will sacrifice whoever comes to greet him first upon returning home if God will help him be victorious. After defeating the Ammonites, Jephthah returns home and is greeted by his only daughter who dances out to meet him. Jephthah is distraught; the scripture tells us he rips his clothes—a sign of deepest grief. But he does not take responsibility for this horrible turn of events; he instead responds by blaming his daughter: "Alas, my daughter! You have brought me very low; you have become the cause of great trouble to me. For I have opened my mouth to the Lord, and I cannot take back my vow" (Judg. 11:35). As the religious ideal of a self-sacrificing, obedient female, she responds by accepting the consequences of her father's vow. She says, "My father, if you have opened your mouth to the Lord, do to me according to what has gone out of your mouth" (Judg. 11:36). Yet, she does ask for two months to "wander on the mountains, and bewail my virginity, my companions and I" (Judg. 11:37). This story raises questions about how her companions or friends (as I imagine them) played a role in her decision. That is, just as *The Red Tent* provided an alternative backstory to some of the key women of Genesis, so we might do the same in this case.

Such inquiry might even change our reading of the passage. Biblical scholars have debated whether the daughter would have known of her father's (Jephthah's) promise. Danna Nolan Fewell writes, "Jephthah's vow was most likely made at Mizpah and not necessarily in secret. The daughter could very well have known the substance of her father's bargain. Indeed, when she responds to her father she seems quite aware of what the vow entails."[3] In that case, her response might not be one of submission, but judgment. As Fewell contends, Jephthah probably wanted his daughter to know about the vow so that she would not come to greet him and he could sacrifice a servant. If that is true, then "the daughter intends her greeting. She is one of Jephthah's troublers because, as she steps forth, she takes the place of someone whom he has considered expendable."[4] Whether knowingly or not, the daughter places herself in a position of self-sacrifice. In the reading offered by Fewell, however, she does so to save another, less valued member of the household by using her limited power in a patriarchal context. She is also the one who requests the two months to be with her companions and mourn her womanhood (presumably away from men, or at least, her father). The Bible does not record who these companions were. But based on gender customs and her age, I would guess it was her girlfriends and other female servants.

With no social or religious power as a young woman in her time, I wonder if the love and support of her friendships sustain her in her decision to save other members of the household (assuming Fewell's reading is correct) and reveal her father's (and perhaps also the Bible's) prioritization of military victory and of male lives over those of women. After all, when Abraham pleads for Isaac's life, God does not require Abraham to fulfill the sacrifice of his only son. Jephthah seems only to call on God when needed for fighting. Fewell suggests, "Yahweh is merely another party to be bargained with, and once the victory is granted, to be dispensed with, like the daughter."[5]

What might such a gruesome story of violence teach us about women's friendship? The daughter's world, much like our own to varying degrees, supports gender inequality and perpetuates violence against women. Given customary gendered divisions in the household, Jephthah's daughter probably created relationships with other women and girls, including servants or other members of her extended family. In the case of "friendships" with servants, these women would have been bound together involuntarily because of their social roles and gender. While putting a bunch of women or girls together does not mean they will invariably become friends, I suspect that anyone willing to sacrifice her life for another (as the daughter was for the servants in Fewell's reading) must have had a deep bond and love that may have been tantamount to friendship. In any event, in her period of mourning, her friends probably surrounded her with support and love as they joined her in her wandering the mountains and momentarily made her feel safe and empowered even with the foreknowledge that she would soon experience a violent death.

I imagine that this two-month reprieve gave these women time to bond, mourn, celebrate, and lament away from the confines of male control. (This is not to imply that the mountains provided physical safety. I can't even imagine what kind of animals or natural feats these women dealt with while wandering for two months.) Here we can see how tenuous forming women's friendships can be. Wandering together may have allowed these young women to experience much more than the narrowly defined roles society proscribed for them due to their sex, class, age, and so forth, for a short period of time. But the price they had to pay for this temporary freedom was the risk of either being shunned by the community upon their return, or at least held under suspicion for the time they spent with her in the mountains. These factors might explain why they all chose to return. Every time I read this story, I wonder why they didn't just stay up in the mountains. I have concluded, however, that Jephthah would no doubt have found them eventually and then perhaps killed them all to fulfill his vow and demonstrate the consequences for disobedience.

Often women are pitted against each other. Hopefully, many of us do not face violence or the threat of violence as recorded in Judges concerning Jephthah's daughter. Nonetheless, even the everyday experiences of women make it more difficult for them to form true friendships based on mutual interest, support, integrity, and loyalty. To be fair, there does not have to be a male around to set the stage for jealousy. Females can be their own worst enemies. When dissected, however, this behavior is often a product of internalizing negative stereotypes about women that favor men. As the companions of Jephthah's daughter return with her for her to be sacrificed by her own father, we see that their actions do not change the status of women but ultimately reinforce male rule—and that may tell us more about the writer of the text and community norms at that time than it does about the daughter, her companions or any internalized misogyny on their part. It can be difficult for women to learn to love themselves and each other in a context that devalues them. As a counter-narrative to the devaluation of women, the daughter willingly meets her father to save other female companions. In return, they support her on her journey to take what time they had to create sacred space.

Women's friendship: Entering the sacred chamber

Yes, women's friendships can be difficult to form when male suspicion, lack of safety, and prescribed gender roles keep us from knowing and affirming that we are integral to each other's flourishing as well as recognizing the divine in one another. It took me years to discover this truth. First, I had to come to a point where I could love myself for who I was and am. Second, I had to work hard at valuing other women for who they are. I was never quite comfortable with being a "girl" as it was traditionally defined in my Midwestern, white, Catholic context. I was (and still am) strong-willed and stubborn. I preferred to play sports and run with the boys. I was outspoken and smart. I loved myself, but not as a girl or woman. Relationships with other girls seemed competitive on an undefined playing field, catty and mean, and also second-class in relation to the power boys had on the playground, in the classroom, and in the home. Though I am cisgender, I found being a girl a strange state of affairs.

I attended Roman Catholic schools through high school. Religion and faith experiences were part of my education and my way of understanding the world. My Catholic context in multiple ways reinforced the message that women are somehow different, in a lesser sort of way. I often received inadequate answers to my questions about why women could not be priests. There was usually some reference to Jesus being male and God being our Father. Such a response makes it difficult to see the presence of God—*imago dei*—in the feminine. I was confused when the boys were allowed to behave in one way, while girls' activities were restricted. For example, in second grade, one of the nuns called my mother to report that I was playing too often and too rough with the boys on the playground. So, my mother asked me to spend more time with the girls in my class. I obliged, and joined the girls' circle, following prescribed gender stereotypes for play. The next week the same nun reprimanded me on the playground for standing around, talking with the girls. These new "friendships" were suddenly suspect and the teacher wanted once again to control them. The message "God loves everyone as they are" was in constant tension with religiously enforced standards of gender performance in my experience.

My struggle seeing other women "as friends, as myself" came into stark relief during my high school years as I entered an all-girls high school. In my freshman year I did everything "right." I was part of clubs, made the athletic teams, took honor classes, hung out with the popular crowd, and so on. The girls I befriended were on the same sport teams, in honors classes, and had socioeconomic family structures that matched mine. There were times these cliques turned mean and I was hurt. There were also times that I acted in line with the group and hurt others. None of it seemed like the real *me*—the *me* I now know God was and is calling me to be.

The conundrum of an all-girls environment encouraged girls to be independent on the one hand, but it still perpetuated gendered standards on the other. As a teenager, I distinctly remember receiving both the message that girls alone could do anything *and* that I ought to find a boyfriend. I was proud of having received gender-specific education, yet I knew its merit was partly based on the notion that girls would not do as well with boys in the classroom. These mixed messages vexed me. Over time, I came to realize that my classmates and I were struggling against and measuring each other by invisible, yet very patriarchal, standards.

There is a way that learning to love ourselves and other women can be difficult in social and religious settings that are fearful of sexuality and bent on maintaining a male/female hierarchy. I am not saying that female friendships are somehow necessarily sexualized or that the love commandment implies that kind of love. Some women engage in sexual behaviors with one another and others do not. Rather, there is an embodied connection and deeply felt desire in friendships (regardless of the gender or sexual orientations of the two persons involved) that is present in the sacred space that we as Christians do not regularly name.[6] For example, the love I feel for my children is not a distant, rationalized Christian love of neighbor. It is an erotic connection filled with hugs and kisses, laughter and tears, touch and desire—a deep, gut-wrenching desire for their happiness and well-being as well as hope for their future and pride in their accomplishments. I feel love like that for some of my friends as well. It seems almost taboo to talk about women's friendship this way because many mainstream movies portray this kind of connection between women as a voyeuristic fantasy of straight men.

I even wondered on reading Jephthah's daughter's story why the author makes such a big deal about her virginity. Maybe she loved other women and going to the mountains was a way for her to say goodbye to her beloved? Or maybe a few male guards accompanied the young women and she had sex with one of them? Or maybe she herself didn't care whether she would die a virgin or not. Who knows? And why should it matter? Seeing women only as sexual objects makes it increasingly difficult to love one's self as a woman and love one's women friends free of the measuring stick of sexualized categories that validate women based on their connection to men.

It wasn't until I met women who represented stark differences from me that I was able to really appreciate strong, gifted women made in God's image. This may be why I am drawn to the story of Jephthah's daughter as she must have formed friendships across socially unacceptable lines and had to work very hard to earn the trust of other women. I had to overcome the embedded fear of women's power, other's and my own, that the church and society was trying hard to suppress. In particular, I have had two friendships with women that have taught me about sacred space.

In high school, I met Jessica. Our friendship started out because we were in lots of classes together. We didn't have much in common other than our Roman Catholic faith and our education. She was Mexican American, and I was a white girl with little experience of inter-racial/ethnic families. I played lots of sports and she found them tedious. She came from a working-class family, while I had a car and never once worried about school tuition or fees. Jessica was not one to directly point out these differences. She had subtle ways of checking my class privilege, like mocking my complaints about the price of gas when I had a car to use. She would at times share little bits of wisdom without being judgmental, like pointing out that receiving an invitation to a popular girl's house couldn't erase the mean things she said about me or others last week. She would remind me that I treated other girls differently when I was dating someone. She had a way of generalizing that made her comments seem wise instead of threatening. In clumsy ways, our friendship, arranged by the circumstance of being assigned as sophomore-year lab partners, enabled us to develop a sacred space where girls from different social locations could become friends against social pressures.

As part of our senior-year service project, we started an afterschool group at Jessica's home church and grade school. This endeavor stretched us both. I was better with kids and programming while Jessica was better with logistical planning and understanding their diverse needs. Over time, we got better at recognizing and talking about how our differences made an impact on each other. We didn't always agree or get along perfectly. But through many experiences, including meeting new friends as we moved away from each other for college, we were able to create a sacred space not just for ourselves but also for others who were different from us by extending our friendship.

Later in my twenties, I met Melanie. We often refer to ourselves as twins. This is confusing for some people because Melanie is African American (remember, I'm white). We met during graduate school in New York City. She is an ordained African Methodist Episcopal preacher and I'm Catholic. The PhD program was small, with only one Latino and two African American women a year ahead of me. I was the only one in the ethics department my year. It is often assumed that PhD students will bond because of similar timing and program given the small size of the group. It is often the case that students of color and women need to stick together as the statistics for completion are against them. The four of us did bond. However, something more developed out of the timely circumstances for Melanie and me.

We were drawn into a relationship with each other through a shared vision of Christian hospitality, our fierce desire to survive a PhD program, and a shared joy in laughter. We invited each other into our families, me with a husband and two children and Melanie with her mother, brother, and extended network of cousins. I learned to value Melanie's penchant for public prayer and abiding support for other students and teachers at school. After experiencing conferences where white senior colleagues spoke first and often, we found ourselves bonding over a new vision of academic life. At other points, we were able to offer each other safe spaces away from the pressures of a graduate program or the judgment of colleagues. My family circumstances meant my time was often unequally divided among family, job, and school. Melanie would tease that I was finishing the program at lightning speed; I was jealous of the time she was able to dedicate to reading and travel. Similar to my relationship with Jessica, we shared how our differences affected each other and we cultivated ways to live beyond the walls they might stereotypically create. I hope our relationship is its own form of witness to women seeing each other and honoring each other for what we are in our differences. Living as God sees us creates sacred space.

Of course, I believe Jessica and Melanie both risked more in being my friend. In both cases, I have more social privilege because of my race, class, and family structure. I did and do work hard to recognize my privilege and know that their friendship to me is a gift that changed me. I suspect working through our differences made our relationships stronger. I can also say, for me, these two relationships transformed what I knew about women and friendship because neither Jessica nor Melanie tried to fit me into a stereotypical "white girl/woman" box. Through the experience, I was better able to be accountable for my social, cultural, and religious privilege.

The image of God in each of us can be difficult to find under the layers of what society expects. A friendship that becomes sacred space opens us to seeing how we and others are the *imago dei*—the image of God as feminine. I have experienced women's friendship as sacred space. As the postcard I mentioned in the beginning says, I learned not only what it meant to let someone into the *sacred chamber of the heart*, but also what it meant to *tread softly there*. This takes courage, vision, and belief that God walks with us.

Sacred chamber, treading softly

Perhaps Jessica and Melanie would tell a different story about how our friendship came to be a sacred space. If Jephthah's daughter or her friends could tell their story, we might hear many, even competing, rich details. For each of us, the particulars are unique. In fact, for other women, a sacred space of friendship might be with someone who is very much like them because they understand how family, communities, and culture affect them personally in a way someone who is very different cannot comprehend. When I meet new women, I have to ask myself if I am meeting each and every one in her uniqueness. Am I inviting God to help me see her or have I already let the stereotype filters generate a false picture of who this woman is? Taking the time to hear first and judge second is not easy. We do not often choose our friends upon first meeting. In many cases, we develop friendships that transform into sacred space because we find shared purpose not just common circumstances.

There is one more biblical example that comes to mind: the women who gather at Jesus's empty tomb. The four Gospel accounts of what happens at the empty tomb differ slightly (Mt. 27–28, Mk 15–16, Lk. 23–24, Jn 19–20). But, in each retelling a group of women were the ones who remained, keeping vigil until Jesus died on the cross. They were also the first to go to the tomb following the ritual Sabbath observation of their Jewish traditions. These women were followers of Jesus for some time. The Gospels tell us that Mary Magdalene, two other Marys and additional women were there to keep vigil. I imagine they knew each other well, but probably not prior to joining Jesus's loyal followers. They would have had to overcome cultural differences among them. Perhaps they negotiated their status in the group based on motherhood, length of time with Jesus, and skills they had to offer.

Their presence within the group of male disciples probably raised suspicion. It still does. Most of our churches do not talk about these women as often as we hear about the male disciples. Remember that since Jesus was tried and convicted as an enemy of the state, anyone following him was at risk, so safety was a daily concern for these women. Through their growing friendship, they transform these circumstances into deep and abiding bonds. We are told that Mary Magdalene and the other Mary (and possibly another woman) risk their lives, *together*, to fulfill their religious ritual duty of anointing the deceased. Regardless of what the male disciples said or what the community might have done, the women were together doing the thing they knew to be right. In their shared mourning and their support and care for one another, they created sacred space together. It is in that moment that the Gospels have them witnessing Jesus's resurrection.

The women at the tomb were able to hear good news in a way no one else did. Their friendship led them to the tomb together, but also opened them to seeing in a new way. They did not need the male disciples to believe them when they returned to share their story. God was with them in a way that would not change regardless of social, cultural, or religious determinations about what women should be like. In an extraordinary moment of transformation, our relationships can become sacred spaces where God dwells and we come to see God in each other. This happened for me in my friendships with Jessica and Melanie.

Friendship is about being able to share in each other's vulnerability, offer the other person authentic critique, experience indulgent, fun survival, and thus, create sacred space. Not all women will become our friends, but there is no good reason why any woman could not. It is difficult work for women to move past the social hierarchies often influenced by racial, ethnic, and class divisions layered with judgments about body image, age, sexuality, and family status. It's time we move past defining our relationships with women by who has the more impressive children or best-looking thighs, who got married first or has a better career—these are patriarchal standards. I wish it had not taken me so long to learn how to nurture and build sacred friendships with other women, but their presence has enriched my life and my encounter with that which is holy. Women's friendships that are sacred space create room for God's in-breaking and outpouring love, as well as, a glimpse of the feminine divine.

Notes

1   This chapter is dedicated to the memory of my friend Jessica Vianes, who passed at age twenty-six. Jessica taught me about women's friendship as a sacred space and continues to bless me with wisdom and support even these many years later.

2   For more about the transformative power of conversations among women, see Elizabeth Hinson-Hasty's chapter on "Girl-talk" in this volume (Chapter 7).

3   Danna Nolan Fewell, "Judges," in *The Women's Bible Commentary*, edited by Carol A. Newsom and Sharon H. Ringe (Louisville, KY: Westminster John Knox, 1998), 77.

4   Fewell, "Judges."

5   Ibid., 78.

6   See Mary Hunt, *Fierce Tenderness: A Feminist Theology of Friendship* (Minneapolis, MN: Augsburg Fortress, 2009).

Blessing ritual for women friends

Timing: Consider using this ritual on the Winter Solstice which is said to mark the anniversary day of Jephthah's daughter's death; or pick a time that marks an important milestone in the life of one or all of the women gathered. The ritual might also mark the end of a weekend trip or gathering of women similar to the group who accompanied Jephthah's daughter in the mountains.

Organization: Every woman brings a similar, commonly used, inexpensive item to be blessed and then exchanged. It adds to the occasion if they are wrapped. To avoid confusion or disappointment, it helps to set a price limit if the items are new and to require everyone bring the same type of thing like pens, coffee mugs, scarf, or a necklace charm. Place all the items on a table and join together in the blessing ritual.

Blessing of friendship

[All]
I call you friend(s).
In low whispers and boisterous laughter,
with uncanny perception and blatant truth-telling,
we transform the mundane into the sacred.

We come together as women, as friends.

[Each person takes a turn to say the following to one other
    woman in the group.]
I see God when you . . . (fill in something specific about the
    woman you are speaking to).
Thank you.
Bless you.
Be you. Woman. Friend.

[All]
We come together as women, as friends.

[After the last woman is blessed, everyone joins together to
  bless the items.]

When I use/wear my [item], I will remember friendship
as sustaining, as sacred,
as God's presence in my life and our world.
When I use/wear my [item], I will pray for (each of) you
as friend, as woman,
as God's presence in my life and our world.

This is sacred space.
In lifting up prayer and witnessing God's love,
with open hearts and supportive presence,
we transform the mundane into the sacred.

*For additional prayers or rituals related specifically to
Jephthah's daughter's narrative, see the Reconstructionist
Rabbinical College site Ritual Well at http://www.ritualwell.
org/ritual/jephthahs-daughter-lament.*

Questions for discussion

1   This chapter discusses various ways patriarchal structures
    impede women as well as inhibit their friendships with
    other women. How have you experienced social, cultural, or
    religious stereotypes of women? In what ways has it affected
    your friendships with them?

2   Kate celebrates two friendships with women she's had that
    have been transformative for her in part because of the
    racial/class/familial/and other differences between them.
    Have you had friendships with other women that have been
    transformative? If yes, what made them so?

3   The author turns to *The Red Tent* to imagine what the
    friendships of the biblical women surrounding Jacob might
    have been like; she also explores what kind of friendships
    Jephthah's daughter had with her companions. What stories
    about women in the Bible inform your understanding of
    women's friendships?

4 A central theological claim in this chapter is that women
   can not only create sacred spaces in their friendships with
   other women, but also see a vision of God as feminine in
   so doing. Have you been able to see a female or feminine
   side of God in your friendships with women? What makes
   friendships "sacred space"?

Suggestions for further reading

Bischoff, Claire E., and Rachel Gaffron, eds. *My Red Couch: And Other Stories on Seeking a Feminist Faith*. Cleveland, OH: Pilgrim Press, 2005.

Hunt, Mary E. *Fierce Tenderness: A Feminist Theology of Friendship*. Minneapolis: Augsburg Fortress Press, 2009.

Weems, Renita J. *Just a Sister Away: A Womanist Vision of Women's Relationships in the Bible*. San Diego, CA: Publishing/Editing Network, 1988.

2

Bed rest stinks
(pregnancy)

Ellen Ott Marshall

One out of every five pregnant women finds herself placed on bed rest. The parameters for the doctors' orders range widely, from partial bed rest for a limited time at home to immobility in the hospital until delivery. The common denominator is a mandate to let go of all of the other things one is doing and become primarily a womb. I was placed on bed rest when I started having contractions during my twenty-fifth week of pregnancy with twins. I spent six weeks mostly in bed at home and one week entirely in bed at the hospital.

Although the idea of being ordered to rest might sound glorious, I found bed rest to be an exceedingly difficult experience. For one thing, I was immediately more occupied by anxiety than activity. When you are first placed on bed rest, you know a lot about the things that need doing that you can't do; and you know very little about the one thing you are now supposed to do: lie in bed. For how long? Flat on my back or on my side? Can I sit up? Get up? Long enough to cook a meal? To take a shower? Like many women, I also faced two looming questions immediately: How do I take care of my first child now? What do I do about my work?

You sort out most of these questions pretty quickly and adopt a new lifestyle. I was incredibly fortunate in many ways. I did not have to worry about losing my job or securing good health care. I had a solid support system, loving spouse, and caring family. My mother came to stay with us and took care of nearly everything, from housework to carpool to companionship. I finished my teaching responsibilities that spring semester with the help of colleagues, a speakerphone, and email. I kept up with the necessary announcements from my daughter's preschool and listened to our church services on an iPod. But I was not physically present anywhere outside of our home (except for four days in a Residence Inn when our canyon was evacuated due to forest fire, but that's another story). When you are confined in your home, you are logistically aware of the many things you are missing and you are painfully aware of missing them. From your bed, you watch people come and go. You cannot see the places where they are going or watch them enjoying themselves there. You hear about it. But, you've missed it. And, you *miss* it. You become profoundly aware of the difference between hearing about something and experiencing it yourself. It is the difference between knowing that your daughter is at the playground and actually kissing her sweaty little forehead as she runs from the monkey bars to the slide. Of course, I wanted our daughter, Katherine, to maintain her routine and to have lots of activities and fun, but watching her walk out the door with other people every day was incredibly hard. I was not only sad, but also secretly jealous of all of the wonderful people who were taking care of her when I couldn't.

In hindsight, I see these weeks as a crucible for many of the worries I have as a mother. Pregnancy-related bed rest cast these familiar concerns in a particularly acute way. Will my children be healthy? Have I done something to jeopardize their health and well-being? Will I be able to care for my first child in the ways she needs—and in the ways I want—when these other little ones come along? Will I be able to continue the work and activities that I find meaningful? Will I be able to maintain my professional life? How much will I miss? And what will I *miss*? While lying in bed aware of all of the things I had set down so that the twins could grow, I also had to ask honestly: can I care for these little ones in the way they deserve—and in the ways I want—without becoming resentful about it?

Like many women, I have been shaped by the idea that we demonstrate the depth of our love by the extent of our giving. One of the ways that I communicate love to my children is by actively caring for them, by doing things that they want to do, and by responding to their needs before my own. This is also one of the ways I have experienced love from my own parents. The fact that my mother immediately dropped everything to come help during the bed rest weeks (and beyond) reflects that. When Katherine was seven, she made it plain to me that I had successfully passed this idea on to her, for good or ill. We were out walking on a cold day, and I commented that I had been so focused on getting the kids warmly dressed that I forgot to grab my own coat. To that, Katherine stated matter-of-factly: "That's because you love us so much. You always take care of us and forget about yourself."

During my fifth week of bed rest, I had a phone conversation with a friend of mine. In the course of our talk, she referred to what I was doing (or not doing!) as "the paradigmatic act of love." She was thinking of love as sacrifice for the good of another, and she praised me for literally laying down my life for the health of the twins. At the time, I received this as both praise and as much-needed reassurance. In truth, as one might guess from the preceding paragraphs, I did not feel very loving. Of course, I loved the twins, and I was genuinely, fully committed to doing whatever I needed to do to bring them as close to term as possible. But I did not feel like someone performing a gracious, voluntary, and beautiful act of self-giving love. I felt ugly and uncomfortable, resentful and anxious, occasionally depressed and angry, and terribly sensitive. I can chalk some of this rollercoaster of emotions up to hormones! But there was also a lot of raw truth in them. Strong emotions, whether amplified by raging hormones or not, are related to things we strongly value. So, it is important to pay attention to them and see what we can learn. As people of faith, it is also crucial to reflect on God's presence in the midst of tumultuous times. What can something like this teach us about God's activity in our lives?

The following pages explore this tangled mess of emotions and commitments. I have a profound love for my children, a habit of expressing that love in forms of sacrifice, and a belief that there is an important connection between love and self-giving. Yet, I also experience anger when I feel spent, frustration when I fall behind in my work, and anxiety and guilt as I try to balance getting my own work done while also caring for my children. Paying attention to this tangled mess has taught me several things. First, I gained an understanding of sacrificial love that helped me to affirm the loving nature of seven weeks that were dominated by awareness of the things I had given up and missed. Second, these seven weeks continue to serve as a cautionary tale about imbalance and loss of self. To avoid that kind of severe imbalance, I learned to practice self-giving love intentionally and carefully rather than to fall back on habits of self-denial. Finally, bed rest and the ongoing challenges of motherhood have taught me to perceive children as agents of grace who not only need our care, but also restore to us life and love.

Sacrificial love

"This is my commandment, that you love one another as I have loved you. No one has greater love than this, to lay down one's life for one's friends" (Jn 15:12-13). In the Gospel according to John, Jesus includes this teaching in a series of lessons that he gave his disciples on the eve of his crucifixion. He calls them "friends" now rather than "servants" because he has shared with them everything he has heard from God (Jn 15:15). Through this series of lessons and the ritual acts of foot washing and of the feast, Jesus prepares the disciples to make sense of his impending death as a form of loving sacrifice for them; he also calls them into a life of ministry that is also shaped by sacrificial love. But of course, the love commandment extends to all followers of Christ, not just those who were there in the Upper Room. We are called to love one another as Christ loves us, and Christ-like love is sacrificial love.

Now, I assume that this is a familiar teaching: the idea that love has a sacrificial quality is a dominant theme in the formal and informal education most Christians receive. For example, my own Wesley Study Bible includes a note underneath John 15 to make plain that "ultimately love shows itself not by declarations of affection but by the service we render to the one we profess to love, especially service that inconveniences us or calls for sacrifice." In this sense, my friend was exactly right. Pregnancy-related bed rest is a form of sacrificial love. Out of love for our children, women quite literally lay down our lives so that our babies can use our bodies for growing. It is inconvenient (to put it mildly), and it entails sacrifice (much like parenting).

Like many Christian women, I recognize the centrality of sacrificial love in my faith tradition but remain extremely wary of it. As Christian feminists have demonstrated, one can appeal to sacrifice for all kinds of malevolent purposes. Language of sacrifice can be used to keep people passive in the face of injustice and abuse.

Sacrifice can be glorified or romanticized in ways that obscure our perception of real human suffering and lessen our drive to alleviate it. And sacrifice can become an end in itself such that one focuses on the things she is denying herself rather than the purpose for giving them up. For all of these reasons, I have been uncomfortable with an emphasis on sacrifice in church and cautious about the way I discuss this theme with students. So, it frankly surprised me that sacrificial love became a helpful way to interpret those seven weeks of my life. However, I can tell you precisely when that happened, when this concept that had always made me wary emerged as an affirming message for me.

It was during the seventh and last week of bed rest, when I was in the hospital. I was not able to get out of bed for any reason. I was hooked up to monitors that would periodically detect distress in my womb. When that happened, two nurses would hurry into the room and rearrange my body, often in incredibly awkward and humiliating positions, until the babies' heart rates returned to normal. I was so grateful for all of the people who attended to me, but I still felt filthy and stripped of personhood. Hospitalization steals your identity in so many ways. You wear a nondescript gown, inhabit a generic room, and interact with people who only know you as a patient. And when you are there for pregnancy-related bed rest, it is almost as though you are part of the machinery around you, one more piece of equipment in service to "Baby A" and "Baby B."

On my fifth evening in the hospital, my husband and I were visited by a priest from our church. She brought with her the little communion case that I had only seen in church being handed to the lay Eucharistic visitors, volunteers who would take communion to homebound parishioners each week. Now I was on the receiving end of this gift. At first, it felt awkward to me, and I was self-conscious and nervous. I have never been comfortable with public expressions of piety; and here I was not only in a hospital room, but lying down in a hospital gown, completely unkempt and vulnerable. But then I heard the words "The Lord be with you," and my husband grabbed my hand as we said, "And also with you." I immediately felt a part of something again, reconnected with others and somehow restored to my own sense of self a bit. Then, we reached the part of the liturgy that reads, "This is my body, given for you." Those words had never hit me as profoundly as they did in that moment. "This is my body, given for you." That night, I found myself repeating that

over and over as I lay in bed listening to the monitors and trying
not to move the wrong way. I soon realized that I was not thinking
about the Eucharist any more, but speaking to my children.

This was a profound moment not because I embraced sacrifice,
but because I felt love. I was reminded that Jesus gave over his body
out of love for us, not out of a commitment to sacrifice for its own
sake. When I receive the bread and wine, I feel God's deep and
abiding love for me. Repeating the words, "This is my body, given
for you," helped me to reorient myself appropriately, to see what I
was doing as a willing act of love for my twins. Like Jesus's disciples
in the Upper Room, I was experiencing the lesson that the point is
not sacrifice, but love. In that moment with the communion liturgy
to ground me, bed rest felt like love, not sacrifice. I was willingly
giving my body over to the babies in my womb.

Self-giving love

This religious experience gave me a way to understand bed rest not
only as an important and necessary thing, but also as a holy and
loving act. This insight was incredibly valuable to me at the time
and remains a vital life lesson today. However, the act of laying
down my life for our children engendered another lesson as well. As
I picked up my life again post bed rest and delivery, now with three
children, my time spent on bed rest also served as a helpful reminder
about balance. One of the reasons I felt gloomy during those bed
rest weeks is that my life was wildly out of balance. I was sedentary
instead of active, dependent on others instead of doing my part,
receiving help instead of giving it, and hearing about things instead
of participating in them. I was not doing the things that were core
to my sense of self. My life was so out of balance that I didn't
recognize myself in it anymore. I experienced in a particularly acute
way something that is familiar to most, if not all, caregivers: we
give so much that we lose ourselves. Those of us who believe that
we demonstrate our love by the extent of our service to others are
particularly susceptible to losing our balance in this way. At some
point, we realize that we are not giving freely with a spirit of love,
but meeting the needs of others out of the habit of self-denial.

The irony is that the very concept—sacrificial love—that became
so meaningful on bed rest proves problematic for parenting.

Giving over my body was indeed an act of love, while on bed rest. However, loving three children well now requires a kind of balance that was not possible then. I use the phrase "self-giving love" to distinguish this intentional practice from the habit of self-denial. I do understand self-giving love to be a form of sacrificial love insofar as it entails prioritizing the needs of another. But I also find that the language of "self-giving" invites intentional reflection on the manner, extent, and spirit of one's giving whereas sacrifice connotes a complete gift of self.

Self-giving love is marked by voluntary and intentional acts of service to others. It involves forms of care that require some compromise of one's own preferences and desires. We give our time, attention, our resources, and energy to another person. I do not have in mind grand forms of sacrifice here, but rather the daily acts of accommodation that are part of being a parent. As simply a matter of course, self-giving parents sleep on the floor next to a sick child's bed, put off a task or relaxation in order to help with a puzzle or join the tea party, field questions that are meaningful to the child but exasperating to the parent, listen to kids' music instead of the morning news, miss an outing because a child had a crummy day and feels blue, and allow yet another fort to be constructed in the living room.

Sometimes, we do these things with a free and happy spirit. We experience self-giving love as a happy outpouring, a kind of grace-filled experience of passing on to others the love we feel inside, the time we have to give, and the attention we easily direct their way. But by its nature, self-giving love also means that we still do these things even when we would prefer to do something else. This is why I also think of self-giving as attached to duty or responsibility. I have a duty or responsibility to care for this person in these particular ways even when I would like to be doing something else. The fact that I am ascribing to a duty and fulfilling a responsibility underscores the sense that self-giving behavior is voluntary and intentional. But what distinguishes this form of accommodating behavior from others is that it is driven by love. The sense of duty or responsibility flows from a profound and abiding love.

But, boy, when the forts, puzzles, and tea cups take over the room, when you feel out of touch with the world, when you can't remember the last grown-up movie you saw or the last time you had a night of uninterrupted sleep, when you hear the same question one more time . . . it is so difficult to maintain your sanity, let alone that loving practice of intentional accommodation! Self-giving love requires a remarkable level of attentiveness. You must attend to the other person, the situation, and your own inner workings. Does she really need this right now? Does he need me to do that for him, or can/ should he do it himself? Should I intervene or let them sort this one out? Do I need to take a break before I start screaming at my kids?

I fail to reach that level of attentiveness regularly, as my children and spouse would tell you. I usually err in the direction of over-extending myself and then getting irritated at those I intended to care for. I have learned from my own mistakes that sacrificial love that tips toward self-denial and away from self-giving no longer feels like love. It does not feel like a loving act to me, and it does not feel like loving care to my children. The further I get from intentionally and willingly accommodating to our children, the angrier I get. And I find that I am not only denying my own preferences begrudgingly, but that I am losing myself. Popular psychology has generated volumes of material for women like me, encouraging us to put on our "oxygen mask" first, maintain some reserves, draw some limits and abide by them, and practice self-care. I recognize some truth and good counsel in all of this, and I do know that one of the most loving things I can say to my children is this: "Mommy needs to take a break."

I also know that one of the most loving things that I do for my children each week is to take communion and to pray for the right combination of patience and courage to love my children well. Expending myself out of love for my kids has pushed me to develop my spiritual life in new ways. In other words, parenting exposes my own limitations every day, making plain that I rely on the grace of God to be the mother I strive to be. In the Eucharist, I not only remember the love that drives the giving, but I also feel loved, sustained, and forgiven by God. In the Eucharist, and in the brief moment of calm that I sometimes experience at prayer, I know the grace of God.

Life-restoring love

Fortunately, grace is not only mediated through the Eucharist or at the kneeler in church. In fact, more often than not, the little buggers who are making me crazy also become agents of grace for me. In the early morning hours, our three kids tend to migrate toward our room to pile in "the big bed." So, I often spend the first few minutes of my day, surrounded by my sweet, sleepy children. Sometimes, we talk a little bit about the day. Sometimes, we look for planes outside the bedroom window. Sometimes, we just lie there quietly until someone starts complaining about being squished or someone else being stinky, or until the dog starts barking to go out. But those morning minutes—no matter how few they are or how abruptly they end—are some of the most precious minutes of my life. In those minutes, I feel an overflowing love, exuberant joy, and serene peace all at the same time. No matter what lies ahead that day, no matter what work needs doing, no matter what anxieties are waiting to flood back into my mind—in those minutes, I know love. I know the joy of self-giving love and the gift of life-restoring love. I am restored by the very people to whom I have given something of myself. And I remember something I keep telling myself not to forget: that children are not only recipients of love, but also agents of grace.

In the midst of the chaos, tantrums, and squabbles of a regular day, children manage to mediate God's gracious love. But sometimes, we are so focused on the various forms of giving and doing required to get through the day that we miss the chance to breathe in God's grace, if only for a moment. Seeing children as agents of grace simply means that we pay attention to everything, not just the moments that require something of us. Pay attention to the dance, pay attention to the goofy thing that makes you laugh, pay attention to the surprisingly sweet interaction between brother and sister, pay attention to the pursed lips of a child learning a new thing. Really pay attention, and breathe in deeply. Imagine that you are breathing in this moment of joy, sweetness, love, goodness. Allow yourself to feel sustained by it, to savor it, if just for a moment, and then exhale and get on with the work of parenting again. I find that those little moments have the power to restore my soul. The greatest challenge is not finding those moments, but remembering to be nourished by them.

While working on this chapter, I have been struck by the fact that in my gloomiest weeks and in some of my happiest moments, I have been lying in bed with my children! I mentioned earlier that bed rest was hard because my life was so out of balance. Bed rest was also hard because I completely lost perspective. In my frustration and anxiety, I was not able to see the moments of grace that surrounded me. I see them now, in retrospect: my mom's constant loving care, my friend's visit on a particularly crappy day, my husband's arrival at the hospital each evening with a different Netflix envelope in hand, my daughter's enthusiasm for a wide array of arts, crafts, games, and books that we could do in bed, my colleagues and students who emailed to check in on me, the prayer shawl and crib blankets from our church's knitting ministry. I appreciated these things, of course, but I did not see them as moments of grace and feed off of them as I could have. If I could have seen them, really seen them, I might have experienced not only the work of self-giving love, but also the sustenance of life-restoring love.

Fortunately, my life keeps presenting me with opportunities to get this perspective right. I do not give myself as entirely to the twins as I did during those seven weeks. But as a working mom of three kids with a spouse whose job requires regular travel, I find myself struggling every day just to accomplish the different kinds of work that need doing. Some days, things fall nicely into place. I have a good day in the classroom, nice interactions with students and colleagues, some time to get ready for a meeting, and then get the kids home for a fun supper together, and move cooperatively through the evening routine. But often, the days are rushed and complicated, the evening hosts a fair share of complaints and squabbles, and I am preoccupied by the hours of work I need to do after they go to sleep. Of course, these are the evenings when I really need to employ these lovely spiritual practices I have described and the evenings when I am too exasperated to do it! But if I am lucky, these are also the evenings when I am surprised by the kids: when Katherine jumps in to help out somehow without being asked; when I get an impulsive hug and kiss on the thigh from Zoe; when Stephen gets so tickled by his whoopee cushion that we all start laughing. This habit of self-giving love that I find so meaningful is also somewhat dangerous. If we don't pay attention to the life-restoring love that is also coursing around us, if we miss seeing our children as agents of grace, then we risk forming a disposition that is more giving than loving. Practicing self-giving love requires that we also craft our lives to capture and breathe deeply the moments of grace that restore us.

Breathing exercises

Few of us make the time for meditation, but you can easily integrate "spiritual respiration" into the course of your day. Broaden your understanding of God's grace to include anything that helps you get balanced, anything that makes you smile or settles your nerves, anything that uplifts your spirit a bit. Then, pay attention to the way in which those feelings become known to you, the way in which these forms of grace are mediated to you. When you spot something, focus on it. Pay attention. Breathe deeply. Allow yourself to soak in that thing just for a moment before going on with your work.

Questions for discussion

1 What do you make of Ellen's struggle with the traditional Christian emphasis on sacrificial love, especially for women who are mothers? Do you have similar struggles with the sacrificial language of Christianity?

2 Much of what Ellen describes in her care for her children also applies to caregivers of all kinds. Have you ever felt overwhelmed by your obligations and the amount of sacrifice required that you started to resent your "job" or get irritated at the ones you are caring for? If so, what helped you to feel less resentful or irritated?

3 Do you think Ellen's approach to wholeness might be helpful in your life? Have you also had experiences of grace, or life-restoring love? What strategies of self-care do you employ?

4 Ellen talked about the Eucharist, prayer, and breathing in grace as important spiritual practices for her. Do you have spiritual practices that you keep up and find helpful as you juggle the demands of your life?

Suggestions for further reading

Bischoff, Claire, Elizabeth O'Donnell Gandolfo, and Annie Hardison-Moody, eds. *Parenting as Spiritual Practice and Source for Theology: Mothering Matters.* New York: Palgrave Macmillan, 2017.
Miller-McLemore, Bonnie J. *Also A Mother: Work and Family as Theological Dilemma.* Nashville: Abingdon Press, 1994.
Stensvold, Anne. *A History of Pregnancy in Christianity: From Original Sin to Contemporary Abortion Debates.* New York: Routledge, 2015.

3

The Chuck E. Cheese challenge (*simple living*)

María Teresa Dávila

"Mommy, can I have my birthday party at Chuck E. Cheese?"[1] You might be familiar with this question. It doesn't arise from greed or selfishness, but my daughter has seen the commercials, and wants me to know that she, too, wants what other children her age are experiencing. After all, if it's advertised on a kids' channel it's good and normal? "I want *that* for my birthday!" insists one child watching commercials during the children's favorite TV show. "No, I want it for Christmas! That's coming sooner than my birthday!" says another sitting right beside. At these moments my feelings are many and conflicted: exasperation at the incessant nagging about "stuff"; disappointment that they haven't learned the lessons about simple living that I'm trying to teach; worry that perhaps I am not the best witness to a simpler life; concern about how best to utilize these times as teachable moments; frustration at the advertising industry that barrages our children with ads; and guilt that as a working mother I might not be giving my children enough attention. Just as I begin to wonder if perhaps it would be okay to indulge my children and let them celebrate their birthdays however they desire, the oldest chimes in, "You can't want everything you see on TV. God doesn't want you to want everything." Perhaps our family's commitment to simple living is getting through to them. A mom can only hope!

The journey to simple living began with a single step . . .

Trying to make economic decisions grounded in biblical witness often seems "a feat impossible for humans" (Mk 10:27, NABRE).[2] Before seminary, I had an adequate grasp of key stories in the Bible, but I was unfamiliar with so much of the economic teachings of the prophets or Jesus's Sermon on the Mount. If you had asked me then whether the Bible or my faith had anything to do with the way I consumed, I probably would have said no. Early in my theological education, however, I was moved to connect the Bible stories of the Exodus, prophetic concern for just economic relations in the land, and Jesus's concern for the poor with the way the economy today forces us to make unjust choices.

For instance, I began to see buying secondhand as a means to honor the lives of laborers and care for the environment. This choice was not well received by many around me. There was, and still is, significant stigma around wearing clothes from the Salvation Army or Goodwill. When I "made the switch" to secondhand only I was questioned as to whether this was a sanitary practice, since wearing clothes strangers have worn before is perceived as dirty—something that only homeless people do and a sign of economic need. I have been able to sustain this practice since the children appreciate that I am always "on the hunt" for something fun to wear. The older ones are starting to understand the environmental costs of our demand for cheap clothing from outside the United States, in transportation, poor environmental regulations, and the dangerous working conditions in the factories that produce cheap clothing for US consumption.[3] Will there be a time when advertising and peer pressure will rob me of my ability to pass on secondhand clothing as "new to them"? Probably. But I hope that by then they will know the values that made me choose this practice, aware of who benefits and who pays a high price for our want of "the next new thing," and couple simpler living with their Christian commitments.

In the story of the rich man in the Gospel of Matthew (19:16-23, also in Lk. 18:18-23) the former asks the latter about entering heaven. Jesus's answer is simple: follow the law, the Ten Commandments and the Torah, and the prophets. When the man states that he has already done all this, Jesus says: "If you wish to be perfect, go, sell what you have, and give to the poor, and you will have treasure in Heaven. Then come, follow me." Sometimes I feel that the takeaway from this passage is clear—the path of discipleship requires a simpler life, but more often than not, I feel that "it is easier for a camel to pass through the eye of a needle than for one who is rich to enter the Kingdom of God," a feat impossible for humans, but possible in God's merciful love (Mt. 19:24-26).

A consuming history of my family and some acts of resistance . . .

The real challenge to my commitment to simple living started with the arrival of children. A child enters a family with a seemingly endless list of *needs*. I would wake up in fits of panic over buying the "wrong" security latch. Security and safety are one of parenting's biggest concerns and marketers know that.[4] Add to this our urge to show affection in the most practiced way we know—by buying more stuff: outfits, rattles, bibs, booties, binkies, and more.[5]

Baby showers were a big challenge. My first child, a girl, was adopted and EVERYONE wanted to bring a gift for this child; guests wanted to honor that we had been waiting for a child for so long and that perhaps this child had suffered want and neglect earlier in life. Shower #1 was massive, and I admit I was swept up in the spirit of it all: feeling like the most special mother in the world, that the many gifts were somehow a safeguard to the challenges of parenting, that all the people giving gifts to this baby would somehow be right there with me during the rough times too. We had shower #2 because the new arrival would be a boy and so everything had to change from pink to blue, right? And shower #3 took place because finally we would have a baby infant, with completely different needs than a toddler.

I know that our friends and families meant well and that their gifts were an expression of love. But for me it began to feel obscene and out of control. Couldn't these showers be organized around stuff that people already had that could be passed down? Was all this stuff really necessary? Could I have put on the breaks and channeled the goodwill of friends and family toward helping homeless families? Throughout these early years, I felt these questions twisting and turning in my heart, but I rarely allowed them the volume to significantly impact the gift-giving dynamics among those who love us the most.

Sustaining a just economy in my home is more than simply staying within our means. Parents are charged with training children to interpret and resist the many ways in which media and advertisers try to shape their desires. In an effort to raise them in the ways of discipleship and desire for God, I am greatly challenged by the billion-dollar effort to shift their attention, wants, and desires toward material things.[6] Different strategies and practices will work differently for different families. For example, I learned very early on in my marriage that the giving and receiving of gifts held a very special place in my husband's Italian family. Initially, I had a very critical attitude toward this tradition. Among immigrant families like my husband's, gift-giving can represent an expression of achievement and hard work. Theologically, it is also an expression of care and deep love. I had to learn about the role of gift-giving in my husband's family as well as offer some resistance and education as to the damages of excessive gifting, providing alternatives such as charitable giving and giving gifts of time spent together in lieu of material things. Now most Christmases, the grandparents are encouraged to give of their time while the grandchildren take them out to lunch or an ice cream using their own money.

Since I am in charge of finances in the home, I decide between necessities and splurges. In this role the Gospel calls me to evaluate my "home economics" in a way that is faithful to the economic messages in the Bible, such as simple living, compassion for the poor, good stewardship, and hospitality to the stranger and the marginalized. Matthew 25 confronts me with a final judgment that directly relates faithfulness to the works of mercy: feeding the hungry, clothing the naked, visiting the imprisoned, welcoming the stranger, and comforting the sick. The passage of the rich man and Lazarus (Lk. 16: 19-31) speaks to the wide chasm that is established between us and others in our community when our lives are solely grounded on our riches and our possessions.

In conversations with other parents, I have noticed some similarities among the questions children ask that have an economic impact. You probably have heard some version of these: "When can I have a cell phone? All my friends have one!" or "Can I buy this with my own money?" "I want this now and this other thing for next Christmas," or "Can we eat out at a restaurant tonight?" "When do I start getting an allowance?" and "When are we going to Disney?" Even though my husband and I have committed to living a simple life, it is sometimes difficult for children who live in middle-class, mainstream culture to understand and appreciate why we have chosen to live accordingly and why it is a faithful expression of our love of God and our desire to care for our neighbors. This has been a journey both for us as parents and for our children. We try to note things that are necessities and things that are "extra," often leading to interesting, if sometimes disappointing, conversations from the perspective of our children. When the children note how great they feel when donating or giving of their time we try to reinforce these feelings; we also note how these activities did not require us to spend any money. Much harder are the conversations about money where we try to plan for the future—a vacation, retirement, a special celebration, etc.—because their ability to consider future spending is limited.

As I consider my own journey of faith, another question looms large. Should my home economics guided by Gospel values also have an impact on the political and economic forces around me? It seems to me that contributing to enriching the life of homeless families, for example, must be accompanied by advocacy and activism on behalf of the needs of homeless children in our schools. Reading the parable of the Good Samaritan in Luke 10 tells me that it's not enough to budget charitable giving at church every Sunday. I am confronted with the requirement to cross the road and make a direct impact on the life of the victim left for dead. This has caused many internal struggles as I try to figure out what level of solidarity and activism is appropriate for my family.

I know that simple living as part of the faithfulness of our families has political, cultural, and economic implications beyond the walls of our homes that offer the possibility of improving the lives of all in society. Yet, I struggle as I try to discern what this looks like concretely, in the everyday. I have rarely, if ever, heard a sermon at a church addressing simple living. I am also not too keen to start conversations with other mothers at school on how to plan and schedule opportunities for volunteering. I often find these questions paralyzing and end up throwing my hands in the air resolving to do . . . well, nothing. In the past, some of these conversations with other families have cost us long-standing friendships when they have felt judged by the implications of the topic of simple living or questioned about their economic choices, or because they have not wanted to subject individual consumer habits to public evaluation. Being a family committed to simple living can feel socially alienating—for example, our children have stopped being invited to birthday parties because they brought only homemade gifts and cards and some colleagues have derided the choice to reject career advancement opportunities for the sake of having more time for family and faith. I have slowly learned that these questions are best answered and lived in the context of a community of other families stirred by the challenge of exercising faithful home economics.

It has not been easy to make decisions that limit the constant acquisition of toys, electronics, clothes, and the like. Luck has us celebrating four family birthdays during the summer months, so early on we decided to have only one birthday party for all our children, where guests are asked NOT to bring a gift (please?!) and nobody gets a goody bag when they go home. Some years this has worked out rather well, others not so much. One year, for example, the birthday party included a collection of nonperishable foods for the local food pantry instead of gifts. The kids were excited to see their friends arrive with cans and boxes to be donated and they placed these items in a box that they had spent significant time decorating. In the past, however, inevitably one of the kids would ask me when we were going to open the gifts. Once, a crying fit ensued by a very confused and disappointed child, prompting a massive guilt trip for me, followed by days of questioning whether I had made the right choice. It also took some time to get loved ones on board our "no-gift" approach to birthdays. They often felt slighted by our wishes, as if they were outright forbidden to express their love and joy for our kids. As their families and ours have grown, they now mainly see it as a cost-saving measure that is also practical. It was hard for me to consider that decisions my family had made, informed by faith and the Gospel, were potentially hurtful to others. I therefore try to find allies among my family and friends—as well as blogs, authors, websites—with whom I can check in about these issues.

Do my possessions really get in the way of loving God and loving others?

My growth in understanding discipleship as related to home economics returns to some of the more salient Gospel passages regarding wealth. We are familiar with the contrast between the Rich Man and Lazarus, one dining on sumptuous meals and dressed in finest robes, the other begging at the gates with nothing to eat (Lk. 16:19-31). Their fate in death illustrates the reversal of fortune that is God's justice, giving the highest places of honor to the least and the oppressed, and making those who are first at the table last. Material possessions are seen as an obstacle to faithfulness. The parable of the Rich Fool in Luke 12 has God conversing with someone fully consumed by the care of his material possessions. And yet God rebukes him by reminding him that his life could end any minute, having squandered all of it on material cares and preoccupations rather than rejoicing in the love of God (Lk. 12:16-21). Very clearly we are told that excessive possessions are an obstacle to true faithfulness to God and of experiencing God's love. The multibillion-dollar advertising industry attempts to claim a stake in our children's mind, heart, and soul (and mine as well, since the beauty industry spends over $2 billion in advertising to convince me I'd look awful without them!),[7] occupying the central place that loving God and loving our neighbor ought to have in our lives.

The message toward simple living in the Bible is intimately linked with God's love for the poor. As the rich man in Matthew and Luke was told to sell his possessions and give the proceeds to the poor, we are also told to have special care and a relationship with "the widow, the orphan, and the stranger." When we learn about God's covenant with Israel, care and protection of the poor and vulnerable is highlighted as an expression of a faithful people. In Deuteronomy 14, for example, we hear that our offerings must be at the service of the Levite (the stranger), the widow, and the orphan within our gates, that they may eat and be satisfied (Deut. 14:28-29). This is pleasing to God. By contrast, not extending our generosity to the needy among us is against God's commands: "If one of your kindred is in need in any community . . . you shall not harden your heart nor close your hand against your kin who is in need. Instead, you shall open your hand and generously lend what suffices to meet that need" (Deut. 15:7-8).

Simple living—keeping our consumption under control in a consumer society, teaching our children and ourselves to resist the lure of advertising—is but one side of just home economics. Love and care for the poor, what Christian churches, especially in the Catholic tradition, call the "option for the poor," is the other. It has not been easy to follow the command to love and care for the poor within my family. Three examples show how we in my family have tried to negotiate the Christian call to love neighbor, and unexpected challenges in each. We write Christmas cards to prison inmates through a long-standing peace initiative in Philadelphia. The children love doing the artwork; they understand that all you have to do at Christmas is send someone else God's blessing and love. They also learn that God's love is showered on all, including those whom society has judged as belonging in jail. This activity also teaches them reciprocity, as the inmates send Valentines to the children.

Though I have always wanted to engage in some form of prison ministry, I realize that having a family makes direct contact with inmates a challenge. I have thus wondered what would be safe ways of communicating God's love and our care to inmates while protecting my children as a vulnerable group. While I understand that some of my own concerns about safety result from biases and stereotypes against prisoners, it's been a relief for me to have found an agency that already has a system in place for us to share our love with those in prison while keeping our identities anonymous. Our Christmas card-decorating sessions also offer us an opportunity to have hard conversations about the criminal justice system, prejudices against convicts, and God's forgiveness and mercy.

My church tradition's very organized Lenten solidarity journey (Operation Rice Bowl)[8]—with a complete website, and recipes to follow from different countries—has helped us connect charitable giving and the lives of the poor to prayer and spirituality. The children have enjoyed finding faraway places on the globe as well as watching the videos of what life is like in other countries. It also has become a lesson about waste in our own home as they can't help but think of children carrying buckets of water for miles whenever any of our taps are open longer than needed.

Lastly, I have a long-standing relationship with Housing Families, Inc. As a family we try to make Housing Families the focus of many of our activities, either through getting back-to-school supplies for the families, raising some cash through a yard sale, or volunteering our time. As the children have grown and the political situation has shifted, we have expanded our notion of hospitality and aid to the homeless through opening our home to refugees. The children connect this disposition with the lives of key figures in the Bible and contrast the loving families we have met with some of the portrayals of refugees in the news.

The road ahead

Our commitment to living simply is part of our faith journey, and, as such, it continues to evolve over time. We would like to grow vegetables and fruits as part of practicing justice in what we eat. While we are incredibly conscientious about recycling and composting and we generally limit eating out and gift-giving, growing our own food or even joining a CSA[9] seems impossible with our busy work, school, and travel schedules. In short, for every successful consumption-reducing practice, there are countless examples where we continue to struggle to resist the cultural pressures to consume. This year's back-to-school shopping is one example. Rather than question or negotiate the excessive list of "needs" given by the school, I bought every item on the list—for all four kids going into school! My heart sank when the supply list for one child alone totaled $100. I questioned whether pens of many colors were really a "need," or whether there were ways in which schools could consider asking the kids to make their own notebooks out of recycled paper. I wonder how the PTO would feel about a conversation on environmental and worker justice and how this relates to the infamous school supply list.

Those practices that are successful for us today may not be so in the future. There is no one right answer for how to live faithfully and live simply but I do feel a responsibility to lay the foundations for my children today to help them see how our Christian values regarding money, finances, and home economics continue to evolve and respond to our family's needs and to the changes in the world around us.

Notes

1 The restaurant and entertainment business that includes Chuck E. Cheese, has grown through the years to include food and entertainment choices for older kids and adults. Places like Dave and Busters caters to the pre-teen crowd, and Lucky Strike and King's both focusing on bowling, with full bar and menu choices that keep the adults entertained while a "child's" party takes place at the bowling lanes.

2 In this chapter, Scripture quotations are taken from the New American Bible, revised edition (NABRE) © 2010, 1991, 1986, 1970 Confraternity of Christian Doctrine, Washington, DC, and are used by permission of the copyright owner. All rights reserved.

3 *Overdressed: The Shockingly High Cost of Cheap Fashion* (New York, NY: Penguin Books, 2012) by Elizabeth L. Cline is a great resource for understanding the ethical questions around today's garment and fashion industry.

4 My thorough internet search for the average amount parents spend on baby safety equipment, the so-called process of "baby proofing" a home, yielded listings for hundreds of baby proofing services. These are "professional" companies that will come into your home and assess the items you will need to keep your child safe, such as locks for your cabinets, anchors for furniture that might topple over, and padded corners for objects with right angles. One such company, Childproofers.com, informally reports that "parents spend in excess of $1 billion annually on safety products." http://www.childproofers.com/child-safety-facts/ (accessed February 5, 2018).

5 Two authors who recently discussed the links between parenting and consumption include Pamela Paul, *Parenting, Inc.: How We Are Sold on $800 Strollers, Fetal Education, Baby Sign Language, Sleeping Coaches, Toddler Couture, and Diaper Wipe Warmers—and What It Means for Our Children* (New York: Times Books, 2008); and Alison Pugh, *Longing and Belonging: Parents, Children, and Consumer Culture* (Berkeley, CA: University of California Press, 2009).

6 The Campaign for a Commercial Free Childhood, an organization that works to change practices and policies that control how children are targeted for advertising in television and online media, estimates that "companies spend about $17 billion annually marketing to children." "Marketing to Children Overview," http://www.commercialfreechildhood.org/resource/marketing-children-overview (accessed February 6, 2018). Many marketing campaigns to children

have become increasingly cost effective through the use of social media and Youtube videos. Instagram offers product recommendations that match a person's taste as it follows that person's clicks through the internet and social media platforms (which are often linked to each other). The phenomenon of "unwrapping" videos, where children, even entire families, focus on carefully unwrapping and opening a new toy and showing all its parts gets millions of kids watching this "free" marketing strategy, often unbeknownst to parents (Heather Kelly, "The Bizarre, Lucrative World of 'Unboxing' Videos," *CNN.com* (February 13, 2014), https://www.cnn.com/2014/02/13/tech/web/youtube-unboxing-videos/index.html). This online marketing phenomenon includes kids of all ages up through adults who spend a significant amount of time watching unboxing videos of beauty products and makeup.

7   $2.2 billion were spent in 2005 alone. Hillary Chura, "On Cosmetics: Marketing Rules All," *The New York Times* (November 18, 2006). Available at http://www.nytimes.com/2006/11/18/business/18instincts.html?_r=1.

8   http://www.crsricebowl.org/.

9   CSA stands for Community Supported Agriculture. These are cooperatives that deliver local, organic, and fairly farmed produce directly either to one's home or to a local pick-up site. For more information on the variety of CSA programs available in the United States, visit http://www.localharvest.org/csa/.

An "alternative" commitment and blessing of the home:

Consider the following ritual as opening the door in your home and/or your faith community for conversations and commitment to just home economics.

I Gathering prayer (Sitting together at a kitchen table or in the parish hall, invite all gathered in with a simple prayer of your choice. The goal of the prayer is to invite the Spirit to bless the gathering and open our hearts to God's desire for justice in our homes.)

II Reading of scripture (Depending on the composition of the group—whether there are children present, only mothers, clergy, and lay people—pick a scripture passage discussed in this chapter or another of your choice that challenges us to think differently about how we relate to our possessions and to the poor.)

III Open discussion (Using some of the lists of questions or discussion points in this chapter, engage each other in conversation about how this passage most challenges our daily living. Be sure to allow space for children to express themselves during this time.)

IV Rewriting scripture for our times (read the passage used earlier in the ritual again). This time, invite those present to adapt or add parts of the passage to represent real situations they would encounter today. An example I offer here is the scene of the final judgment in Matthew 25:

> *Then he will say to those on his right, "Come, you who are blessed by my Father. Inherit the kingdom prepared for you from the foundation of the world.*
>
> *For I was laid off and had to resort to your church's food pantry, and your children played with my children while you helped me get food for the week,*
>
> *I was thirsty and close to death in the desert and you helped your church's water ministry for migrants,*
>
> *Knew only a few words in English and you helped me with a job application,*

*At a battered woman's shelter and you brought me
clothes and toiletries,*

*At an old age home and you were part of a choir visit
at Christmas,*

*in prison with a death sentence and you lobbied for
leniency for my life."*

V   Alternative Commitment/Blessing (Using paper, crayons,
    markers, and other creative materials, encourage those
    gathered to write an alternative commitment/blessing on
    the home based on the challenges discussed. For example,
    a commitment can be to cook one simple vegetarian meal
    every week and donate the savings to the church's food
    pantry, with a corresponding blessing of eating healthier,
    connecting with the hands that bring us our produce, and
    offering food to others in need.)

VI   Building a "Blessing on the Home" Mural (Use a song or
     prayer to call all present to build a mural made up of the
     artistic expressions of the commitment/blessing. Be sure
     to include the rewritten version of the scripture passage
     somewhere on the mural.)

VII   Closing prayer (Close with a prayer that is meaningful
      to your community or family. Include in the closing the
      promise to make the mural visible to all and to revisit it and
      its challenges at a later date.)

This ritual can be adjusted to the age level of those present, whether
there are small children or it is part of a church youth group exercise.
It is not meant as a once-in-a-lifetime or even once-a-year event.
Rather, it can be part of the ongoing acknowledgment that this is
a life journey. The rewards and lessons from the choices we make
encourage us to take on different and more challenging projects
while being clearer in our witness of core values we hope to share
with our families moving forward.

Questions for discussion

1   Do you recall in your childhood asking your parents for
    the kinds of things María Teresa (MT) says her kids ask her

for? If you are a parent with school-aged children, are you bombarded (as she is) with requests for material things your kids want to buy, expensive activities they want to do, or costly trips they want to take? What emotions, concerns, or reactions do these memories or questions evoke for you?

2   Have you ever wondered whether what society deems as "necessary" really is? MT, for instance, seems to be implying that clothing is a "need," while their being purchased new (versus secondhand or used) is only a "want" she is willing to dispense with. How do you distinguish "needs" from "wants"? Have you made decisions in your life to forsake things you can otherwise afford to buy for some greater principle? If so, what?

3   MT's chosen path of "simple living" is a countercultural ethic that she describes as grounded in her Christian faith. Do you experience Christianity and the Gospel in particular as calling you to live counterculturally as well, either by "simple living" or something else? If so, what are some of the struggles that you encounter in doing so?

4   Faithfulness to the Gospel according to MT is not only shown through "simple living," but doing the work described in Matthew 25: feeding the hungry, clothing the naked, visiting the imprisoned, welcoming the stranger, and comforting the sick. In what ways are these acts of caring for those in need part of your religious practice or discipleship?

Suggestions for further reading

Day, Keri. *Religious Resistance to Neoliberalism: Womanist and Black Feminist Perspectives*. New York: Palgrave Macmillan, 2015.
Peters, Rebecca Todd. *Solidarity Ethics: Transformation in a Globalized World*. Minneapolis, MN: Fortress Press, 2014.
Rubio, Julie Hanlon. *Family Ethics: Practices for Christians*. Washington, DC: Georgetown University Press, 2010.

4

I want my babies back
(miscarriage)

Monica A. Coleman

I grew up in the 1980s when the biggest public health crisis was a new disease called AIDS. My closest friends and I were trained to be deathly afraid of unprotected sex. At worst, we were told, we could get AIDS and die. At best, a girl could get pregnant and there went her career dreams. This is how "safe sex" was presented to us. Yes, our churches told us, "Don't do *it*, until you are married." But the more compelling reasons came from our health education class in school.

One day after school, two friends and I positioned ourselves in the pharmacy section of our local drugstore, dropping our backpacks to the floor, bending over so we could read the small print on the varied boxes of condoms. We each chipped in some money so we could buy one three-pack of condoms and each of us could carry one condom in our wallets. We had no sexual partners or plans, but this made us "90s women." With a condom tucked into our billfolds, we felt very grown-up.

Thus I never had unprotected you-could-get-pregnant-from-doing-this sex until I was interested in getting pregnant. I was in my mid- to late thirties by then. The downside to being a health educator's dream is that you don't know if you can get pregnant until you try.

My gynecologist said "tick tock" in reference to my biological clock more than a year before my partner and I were ready. We both have friends who have wanted to get pregnant and couldn't. We knew a little about infertility treatments like artificial insemination and in vitro fertilization. My partner wondered if our health insurance covered it. I said that it didn't matter.

All my health decisions are made in consideration of my mental health. I live with a depressive condition—and I had since learned that extra levels of estrogen are very bad for a depressed woman's body. Although not all doctors agree, my experience told me this. I had four horrific weeks on the birth control patch when a doctor thought that was the best solution to my uterine fibroid tumors. I vomited every healthy thing I ate for one week and felt suicidal by week three. I wasn't particularly unhappy, but I found myself thinking about death. It didn't make sense. I stumbled across a book on the nutritional treatment for psychiatric disorders that mentioned how bad estrogen was for depression. It definitely explained why PMS felt so bad. Having previously informed the prescribing doctor of my mental health challenges, I decided that enough was enough. I ripped the patch off my backside and calmly informed the nurse that I would be looking for a new doctor.

If a patch of estrogen jacked me up, I didn't want to find out what shots of it would do. There would be no IVF, no counting days, no taking temperatures, I declared. We would not turn our intimate life into a clinical laboratory.

Of course, these things are simple to say in theory. Decisions in reproductive health, like much of life, are easier made in theory than when one is watching hopes and dreams circle the drain. Who knows what we would do?

We didn't exactly know what we would do when I stopped bleeding. This is what wombs are about, right?

Blood.

Blood made me fear HIV. The sight of blood is a relief if pregnancy is not desired. The sight of blood can mean menstrual cramps. For many women who live with depression, the sight of blood is a relief from the four-day intense depression of PMS.

I could almost set my watch to the hour at the sight of my own blood. When there was no blood, I assumed everything except pregnancy—stress, changing time zones, the high altitude of a transcontinental flight.

I long became comfortable with menstrual bleeding. I read *The Red Tent* by Anita Diamant, *Honoring Menstruation* by Lara Owen, and *Sacred Woman* by Queen Afua. These texts guided me into a healthy relationship with my womanhood, my womb, and the cycles of the moon. I didn't know what to do when I stopped bleeding.

It felt like weeks before I got to a pharmacy, asked if brand name made a difference, and bought not one or two but *three* sticks to pee on. Finally, the lab took my blood to test for the hormone. I wanted to be sure.

I also knew not to get attached, not to get excited, and not to make any plans before I knew for sure. I knew the word "miscarriage" as a child because I knew my mother had miscarried before having me. I knew that the first trimester is dicey. I knew bloodlessness could be stress, time zone changes, or high altitudes. While my partner started calling relatives and making plans, I remained stoic—well, stoic and nauseous.

The day we saw the six-week blip on the ultrasound, I exhaled.
It's real.
It's got a heartbeat.
The doctor gave us a due date.
March 3.
We're having a baby!

The doctor shook our hands, advised tests, and answered questions. The nurses congratulated us. They sent us home with a bag of magazines, pamphlets, and samples of pre-natal vitamins.

That night, for the first time in eight weeks, I bled. And even though the internet said that it could be anything, and the on-call nurse said "70 percent of the time it's nothing"—I knew.

I knew that I should not have gotten excited. I knew I should not have folded, unfolded, and refolded the baby clothes my friend gave me. I knew I should not have talked about it as being the size of a grain of rice. I should not have complained about morning sickness. I knew what blood meant.

The nurse told me to stay in bed until the office opened on Monday. My body was in the bed, but I was on the floor. The rug was pulled out from under my feet. And in my heart. I knew.

Sacrifice?

A lot of religions consider blood to be an appropriate sacrifice to God or gods. In the Hebrew scriptures, the Israelites are often told to offer the fatted lamb on the altar. In a story important for Jews, Christians, and Muslims, Abraham is told to sacrifice his son on the altar—saved only at the last minute by the ram in the bush. In the origins of Passover, the Hebrews are told to place the blood of a lamb on their doorposts so that the angel of death will pass by their houses—a final plague in Moses's leadership out of Egyptian slavery. Each time, blood appeases God.

In most churches of my youth (and too many of my adulthood), the Eucharist is still taken to the words of songs about blood. Here are just three of them:

> Would you be free from the burden of sin?
> There's power in the blood, power in the blood;
> Would you o'er evil a victory win?
> There's wonderful power in the blood
> There is power, wonder-working power in the blood of the
>   Lamb[1]

> What can wash away my sins? Nothing but the blood of Jesus
> What can make me whole again? Nothing but the blood of
>   Jesus
> Oh! precious is the flow, that makes me white as snow
> No other fount I know, Nothing but the blood of Jesus[2]

> The blood that Jesus shed for me, way back on Calvary
> The blood that gives me strength from day to day
> It will never lose its power[3]

Blood is the force of life. Blood is supposed to bring us closer to God. When humanity has erred, God recognizes blood and will forgive. Even the blood of Jesus, replacing the blood of previous animal sacrifices, is the ultimate sacrifice. His blood covers the sins of the world and restores us to right relationship with God. These are the lessons of blood atonement.

In many Christian traditions, these ideas are shared during the Eucharist or "Lord's Supper." Our words describe Jesus's sacrifice of his body and blood as a central part of salvation. Jesus signals his disciples to know this during the Last Supper. This, our liturgies say, is the lesson of the cross. In real life, sacrifices of body and blood are too often the bodies of women and children. Too often, our bodies are the unnumbered casualties of war, rape, domestic and sexual violence. Too often, we are told that it is holy to sacrifice our dreams and ourselves. Like many women religious scholars before me, I recoil at these ideas. I value what Jesus does in the Last Supper. I just prefer my lessons on fellowship, forgiveness, and friendship to come with large loaves of bread—without a side of blood.

Can't I talk to God without the sight of blood? I thought to myself. Miscarriage is bloody.

When my partner and I first learned of the miscarriage, we could barely speak. Our eyes spoke to each other: *We can do it again. We can do this again.*

But when I put my foot in a church, I cried. In the safety of my faith community, in proximity of the wooden altar where my prayers had found solace . . . the moment someone asked how I was doing and seemed to really want to know, I bawled. I fell into a heap on the floor, and I bawled.

The next day, my partner and I went to another church service. We sang, we laughed, we cuddled. They baptized a baby—and I bawled. With snot running down my face, my partner's arms tightly around me, I cried again.

We whispered to one another, *We can do it again. We can do it again.*

But I had stopped bleeding. I bled enough to reduce the heartbeat. I bled enough to reduce the size of the little-grain-of-rice baby. But I did not bleed enough to fully miscarry.

At the next ultrasound, the doctor said it almost under his breath: "Two sacs. Twin gestation."

He made some notes on the paper. We asked him to repeat what he said.

"Twins?" we said aloud. We really wanted twins. Both our mothers are twins. We really, *really* wanted twins.

Can we do *that* again?

This enough-but-not-enough blood loss was a sacrifice I didn't want to make. A sacrifice I did not choose. I was no Abraham laying my firstborn before God. Nor were any sins being forgiven.

Our babies were laid on the altars of "I don't know why" and "sometimes it happens" and "it doesn't matter why."

It didn't make me angry with God. But it didn't draw me any closer either.

Activism revisited

I grew up in a state of unionized workers. My mother was in a teachers' union. My father worked for one of the "Big Three" American automakers, and every Michigander knows the acronym UAW (United Auto Workers). Every year, there were talks of negotiations and talks of strikes. The only thing worse than buying "a foreign car" is crossing the strike line.

My babies went on strike. They held up signs in my uterus and said "Hell no, we won't go."

When my friend described the miscarriage this way, I laughed out loud.

For the first time in weeks.

I laughed.

They come by it honestly, she told me. They get this from you and your partner. "Didn't you know," she said while I giggled, "that you would have activist babies?!"

So we waited. We waited for the babies to let go and bleed out.

But they stayed put.

For weeks.

The doctor said he wanted to see if I would bleed. He wanted the miscarriage to happen naturally.

I'm not sure the word "natural" is right.

I was pregnant with non-babies who were on strike. I had all the hormones and the swollen breasts that wouldn't fit into my bras. I had the nausea, but this time with pain.

We waited. For weeks. For my activist babies to throw in the towel.

I lacked the energy to go to church.

I stayed in bed.

At night, in the morning, in the day, my partner and I huddled together, crying, not crying, talking, not talking.

Sad.

Picturing, asking, pleading, acupuncturing. We even tried a nasty-tasting-Chinese-herbal-tea. Begging the blood to come.

Let go, I begged the babies.
Bleed, I commanded my body. Yes, I asked my body to bleed.

Pregnancy and depression

I wanted to be pregnant in part for the possibility of helpful hormones. "Pregnancy is great for some women with depression," my psychiatrist says. "The hormones can help."

But I think of my women friends with depression who tell me that pregnancy nearly killed them; that depression was only alleviated by taking their medication and hoping everything would be okay; that they love their children, but hell if they'd ever get pregnant again.

Medication-free, I rely on strict sleeping hours, a careful diet, and daily exercise to be the brighter side of human. Skip one of those for a day, and depression erupts into my life like a Jenga puzzle tumbling down.

I curse my fragility. I swear that there are normal people out there who don't have to do so much. I rail at God for making my life so complicated, so difficult, so precarious.[4]

Even with these three ingredients firmly in place, they take me to mid-afternoon. As complicated as my relationship with medicine is, I begin to worship the pills that would give my un-conceived children ten heads. Okay, I exaggerate, not ten heads; but no guarantee on developed lungs, heart, and brain.

My psychiatrist checks in: "How is it? How are you doing?"

"It's hard." I replied. And that's the good version.

I have read the bad version. Nearly ten years ago, I went on a quest for camaraderie. I headed to the bookstore and read every memoir on living with depression that I could find. Nothing scared me more than motherhood with depression. I read wonderfully written books like *Sometimes Mommy Gets Angry* by Bebe Moore Campbell, *The Beast* and *The Ghost in the House* by Tracy Thompson, *Beyond Blue* by Therese Borchard and essays whose titles and authors I now forget.

- What if I have no pregnancy glow?
- What if the hormones make me suicidal?
- Will I have to choose between the potential health of my unborn babies and my life?

- Will I be able to take care of babies?
- Will the sleeplessness and responsibility send me to some dark place?
- Will my children be scarred because I lie in bed all day and can't get up to take care of them?
- Will electroconvulsive therapy be the only thing that can cure me? If so, what about the side effect of memory loss? Will I forget the birth, my childhood stories, my grandparents?
- Will I be so sick that I'd happily surrender my memories?

Postpartum depression could kick my ass! If I only make it that far. *Did I really want this?*

On the other hand, I want children. I snuggle next to my partner and say "Babies!" And we get big Cheshire cat grins on our faces. Even in the midst of the no-bleeding-lost-babies, we dream of other children.

I'm a Mama's girl. I have a great Mama! She understands me; knows how to take care of me; checks on me; gives me soft cotton socks; lets me lie to her and say "I'm fine," when her gut tells her I'm not. She knows when to butt in, and when not to. She wears imperfection like grace, and gives love and affection like a rainstorm. When I think about following her example, I am not afraid.

I face the prospect of motherhood with a mixture of confidence and terror. I assume that these feelings won't go away for a long time. I try to make peace with extremes and contradictions.

Until the doctor says that we can try again.

Robbed

"Life is robbery."

I reread this quotation by the philosopher Alfred North Whitehead to my graduate students as we read through his book *Adventures of Ideas*.

I explained that this is one of Whitehead's more frequently cited sentences because he succinctly and poetically describes his position that life entails loss, and you can't go back and get what you lose.

I said the same thing to one of my girlfriends as we chatted in my kitchen several weeks later. I was cooking and catching up with a friend I had not seen in nearly twenty years. As we chronicled our lives from the intervening decades, my friend said: "I have a religious question."

In moments like these, I curse the fact that even my closest friends think that I know the mysteries of God and life because I am a minister and professional theologian. I took a deep breath because that phrase usually precedes some difficult, heart-wrenching question that has no satisfying answer.

"Sure," I replied.

My friend began to talk about some difficult events in her past, and some of what she lost as she wrestled with her own challenges. "Do you think," she asked me, "that we can go back and get what we lost? Do we get a second chance?"

I echoed Whitehead and told her that we can't go back in time. We can't reach back and wrest out what has been lost. Sometimes that is good because this is how we can move past—and even eliminate—some of the worst things in the world. But when we lose things we'd rather not have lost, we don't get them back. I echoed my teaching moment by saying, "That's why the philosopher I study says, 'Life is robbery.'"

But we get second chances. And third and fourth ones. God never stops calling us. As we move forward, there are new opportunities. It's not the same, but we get more chances—often in ways we don't expect.

I know it didn't make her feel any better.

We were quiet for a while and continued cleaning the kitchen and stirring the pot of soup together. We broke the silence by moving to discussions of our future. We talked about how we might live, love, and grow. We laughed about how we were closer to being parents than kids and how that transition sneaked up on us. Then she asked the question I often hear these days:

"So what do you want? A boy or a girl."

I paused. After miscarrying, I've come to understand the answer I've often heard others say: "I just want a healthy baby." But I didn't say that. Perhaps it was the length of our acquaintance, the comfort of the kitchen, or the recent evocation of Whitehead that made me tell her the truth.

"I want my babies back!"

It had been five months since my partner and I saw the bleep on the ultrasound. In the four months after that, I saw my OB/GYN, hematologist, nurses, and anesthesiologist more times than I'd ever wanted to. While I have an intellectual level of gratitude for trustworthy practitioners, good health coverage, and supportive friends, none of it actually gets me what I want. I want the twins the doctor mentioned under his breath from the space between my legs. I want the babies that my partner kept kissing in a place a little higher on my stomach than where they really were, kissing from the moment we realized my period was late. I want the babies about whom I called my mother—even before the official test came back. I want the growing belly, nausea, maternity clothes, and upcoming parental leave.

I deeply believe what I told my friend about second chances, but right now, that means nothing. Grief renders hope philosophical. Grief smothers my ability to think, reason, and plan. Since my honest moment in the kitchen, grief has robbed my life of a measure of joy. *Life* broke into the house of my body and soul and took something that cannot be recovered. There's no one to blame. It just happens sometimes.

And I'll cry about it . . . I guess, until I don't.

Barren woman Bible

I know that men wrote the Bible. That's no surprise to anyone who has had a brush with feminism or biblical scholarship, but there are times when one is more aware of this than at other times. As I mourn the loss of my miscarried babies, I think of how the Bible tells the stories of "barren women."

When I read about Sarai, Leah, Rachel, Hannah, and Elizabeth, the story is always the same. The woman cannot have children.

Like a choose-your-own-adventure novel, the story goes like this:

Option A: You give your husband your maidservant, who then gives him a male child or two or three, and then later God opens your womb so you can bear a male child yourself.

OR Option B: You pray to God about how much you want children, and then later God opens your womb so you can bear a male child yourself.

You end up on the same page at the end: the male child becomes an important religious leader.

As if!

First of all, it's hard to know much about a biblical woman's barrenness. Perhaps they had children, but they were all girls, and only boys "really counted" to the biblical writers. Perhaps the women could get pregnant, but they always miscarried. Maybe they were never able to get pregnant. In the Bible, it's always the woman's problem. But if one chose option B, there's no way to know which attempting parent bore biological responsibility.

In any event, it's too neat. The women cry out to God—or scoff God as in Sarai's case (which is very understandable for a ninety-year-old woman)—and God *makes it happen*. The women thank God for the male child and salvation history continues, happily ever after.

In real life, "barrenness" is much more complicated. It's infertility and miscarriages. It's bleeding and not-bleeding—but on the opposite schedule than you want. It's counting days, doctor visits, peeing on sticks, taking blood, running tests, more doctor's visits and a slew of bills, and—if you're lucky enough—insurance forms. And did I mention what it does to sex?! What was once fun and adventurous can become calculated, programmed, or halted.

And then there's the ending. In real life, God's "fix" is not always a boy-prophet. Sometimes it's adoption. Sometimes it's a birthed-child. Sometimes it's nieces and nephews. Sometimes it's peace with being childless. Sometimes it's a decision not to be a parent at all.

At least that's how it is for me—and the other women who I talk with. But that's the other thing. In real life, there are other women. One in five pregnancies ends in miscarriage. There are other women.[5]

After I miscarried, the women came.

- One sister-friend let me sleep on her bed between doctor's appointments. She took my midnight texts when I asked her, "But what do I do about the grief?" Having miscarried twice herself, she knew that grief came in the middle of the night.

- My play-sister looked at pictures of every pregnancy test— helping me to decipher how many lines I saw.

- Another sister-friend found a free festival in my neighborhood, dragging me out of the bed and into the light of day.
- Another sister-friend brought two days' worth of dinner for my family.
- My mother drew me a bath, knelt on the bathroom floor and washed my hair.

If women wrote the Bible, it might mention how messy the enterprise of not-having-children really is. It might mention the girl children the women loved. It might talk about how the men were in the temple, while the bleeding women gathered somewhere else. If women wrote the Bible, we would have more than these solitary scenes where a woman pours out her heart to God, and God fixes it by "opening her womb."

If this woman wrote the Bible, I'd write about barren women . . . and the women who support them. Those stories would be my love letter to them.

Remembering

We had gotten a due date.

When I had stopped bleeding. When I had peed on the stick. When I had gone to the lab for the blood test. When my partner and I had held hands in the doctor's office. When the ultrasound had showed a tiny circle and a flashing light the OB called a heartbeat.

We had gotten a due date.

And so we had started planning: when I would take parental leave, how we would arrange our finances, where in the house the babies would go.

Had I not bled, had they developed as planned, had I not miscarried . . . our babies would have been born in early March.

The babies would have had headfuls of wavy black hair, like I did. I would have carefully shaped their soft heads, like my Mama did mine. They would have fussed and burped and nursed and cried and slept and made faces that I would swear were smiles and giggles.

My partner and I would have been tired from lack of sleep. We would have dressed them in coordinating clothes. We would have done laundry every day. We would have been happy with the names we had chosen. We would have taken a million pictures and emailed them to friends and family. We would have hosted the grandmothers. We would have had a new rocking chair—maybe two.

We would have had twins.

I remember the due date.

I don't remember the date the doctor said we had conceived. I don't remember the date he printed off the ultrasound picture that looks nothing like a baby. I don't even remember the date I bled, or the date he confirmed the miscarriage.

I remember the date my babies were due.

I think I'm supposed to remember. In the midst of going to work, I should remember. In the midst of making dinner and cleaning the house, I should remember. In the midst of loving other children (one I have since birthed after my miscarriage and those birthed by my sister-friends), I should remember. In the midst of forward-looking hopes and plans, I should remember.

I appreciate that I come from religious traditions that value memory. In the fourth chapter of Joshua, Joshua tells representatives from the twelve tribes of Israel to place a stone from the Jordan River at their campsite. One day, Joshua says, their children will ask what these stones mean and they should tell them about their crossing over the Jordan River and God's delivering them. In Passover meals, Jewish people retell the story of how God brought them out of bondage and into liberation. In the Christian celebration of Holy Week where we remember the passion story of Jesus, we are reminded that how we die says something about how we live and how we should be remembered. In more ordinary rituals, we light candles, we eat bread, and we sing songs to remember people and events that happened generations before us.

I think I am supposed to remember.

I wonder if I should put stones near my front door. Have a meal and talk of my loss? Bake a cupcake with a candle every year? I mention this to another friend who has miscarried. Our due dates are close—although different years. Our babies would have been friends. "Play cousins," we say with smiles and teary eyes. We agree that we should do something to remember them.

Because we don't forget. Being a great "auntie" or having children in the future doesn't replace what was lost. I know in my heart that I have to remember. I'm supposed to remember that even though these babies didn't make it . . . they are still mine.

Notes

1 "There is Power in the Blood," lyrics by Lewis E. Jones.

2 "What Can Wash Away My Sin," lyrics by Robert E. Lowry.

3 "The Blood Will Never Lose Its Power," lyrics by Andraé Crouch.

4 See Gina Messina's chapter in this volume on infertility, "Cursing God," for a comparable expression of anger at God (Chapter 8).

5 See Elizabeth Hinson-Hasty's reflections in this volume on the ways in which other women (through "girl-talk" and "gossip") helped her through her painful experience of miscarriage (Chapter 7).

Prayer

God of Sarai, Leah and Rachel
God of Hannah and Elizabeth
God who hears the whispered hopes and dreams of your
    daughters
Guide and comfort those who have lost life from their wombs
Uplift and sustain those who offer care
Hear our prayers, dry our tears, hold us as we tremble
Remind us that our bodies are temples, our blood is sacred, and
    that our stories matter to you.
Grant us peace about our experiences and grace for the journey
    ahead.
Amen

Questions for discussion

1 Monica's chapter relates the ways that society and church
   teachings have talked about blood, pregnancy, and
   menstruation. What lessons have you learned from your family
   and your faith tradition about women's menstruation? Do
   these lessons include silence, shame, secrecy, ritual, honor, or
   sacrifice? What theological meaning do you ascribe to them?

2 About 20 to 30 percent of pregnancies end in miscarriage.
   Have you or someone you know had a miscarriage?
   Consider the ways Monica talks about her women friends in
   particular supporting her after her miscarriage. What do you
   think women need after miscarriages? How can you support
   others who have gone through this painful experience?

3 What does it mean for your understanding of God to embrace
   the idea that "life is robbery?" How do you feel about the
   tension between thinking that "life is robbery" and the possibility of second (and third and fourth) chances? What might
   this mean for various experiences in your own life?

4 In drawing our attention to the fact that men wrote the
   Bible and that the Bible was produced under conditions of
   patriarchy (as Kate Ott does in chapter 1), Monica notes

that the stories of "barren" women crying out for (male) children might be incomplete. What do you think about the fact that men wrote the Bible? What stories of our foremothers in the faith can you imagine might be missing from our sacred text? How might you fill in the gaps?

Suggestions for further reading

Brock, Rita Nakashima, and Rebecca Ann Parker. *Proverbs of Ashes: Violence, Redemptive Suffering, and the Search for What Saves Us.* Boston: Beacon Press, 2001.

Pence Frantz, Nadine, and Mary T. Stemming, *Hope Deferred: Heart-Healing Reflections on Reproductive Loss.* Eugene, OR: Wipf and Stock, 2010.

Townes, Emilie, ed. *A Troubling in My Soul: Womanist Perspectives on Evil and Suffering.* Maryknoll, NY: Orbis Books, 1993.

5

"Where are you REALLY from?" *(racism)*

Grace Ji-Sun Kim

There was a harsh cold winter in 1975 in London, Ontario. My family had immigrated from Korea that January, and I began kindergarten in the middle of the school year. Everything—the language, the culture, the weather, the school, the teacher, and the country—was new to me and terrifying. I had never seen so much snow in all my life! Walking to school was a feat because I literally got stuck walking in the waist deep snow: I would often take steps and lose one of my boots and then have to go back and pull it out of the snow. It was a cold, bitter winter that went bone deep. On top of that, I had left behind everything that was familiar to me. I lost the "playful" dates with my cousins. I lost my aunts, uncles, and grandparents who spoiled me. I lost the familiarity of my house, neighborhood, and home country and entered a strange new land, which proved to be unwelcoming. While there were many difficulties to work through in my new home, the most challenging was figuring out how to deal with the racism I encountered.

By the third day of school, I had already determined that I hated it. Can you imagine hating kindergarten? What could possibly be bad about crayons and blocks and numbers and cookies and naps? For me, however, kindergarten was more about my classmates taunting and making fun of me because I looked different and couldn't yet speak English. Most of the kids were white with brown or blonde hair and fair skin. I had short black hair with a yellowish complexion. My eyes were brown, with the distinctive epicanthic fold (i.e., "monolid"), and I was physically smaller than my peers. My nose was flatter, my clothes were from Korea and were apparently not as stylish as those of the white kids in my class. My classmates had never met anyone like me. I remember some of the kids asking me during recess "What are you?" I would answer "I am Korean."

They would ask "What is a Korean? Are you Chinese or Japanese?"

I would answer "Korean."

These children had never heard of Korea; they didn't know who Koreans were and thus thought I was making it all up. They were only five or six years old but they often glared at me with disgust and disapproval.

Early on, the language barrier kept me from making friends. It was one thing to be confused, disoriented, and ignorant of what others were saying about me, but with my gradual learning of the language came the pain of finding out just what it was the kids were saying. Some kids were nice, but unfortunately I remember the mean ones the most. Their taunts from the school yard, *"ching, chong, ching chong"* still haunt me today.

The teachers ignored my situation. Or perhaps they didn't notice or, worse yet, they just didn't care what was happening between my classmates and me. To these kids, I was alien, no more, no less. I did not know why they would make those taunting sounds to me. I wanted to lash out at them and say, "Hey. . . . I know how to speak English . . . please just stop that."

I became very shy, quiet, and scared to let others see the terror in my heart. I protected myself and tried to shut out the new world all around me. My terror was so deep that I was unable to share the pain with anyone, not even to my own parents. To this day, they do not know the depth of the pain of those earliest childhood years. Of course, some of this has to do with the culture of shame present in many Asian cultures that makes it taboo to reveal one's experiences of pain, humiliation, or hardship. My parents, family, and culture taught me to keep it all inside and show the world around me that everything was okay. We were not supposed to display anything but courage in the face of pressures from the world.

Survival strategies

The immigrant experience is often very difficult, even for children who often seem so "adaptable." What helped me to survive was having a community of Korean immigrant friends. About fifteen recent Korean immigrant families lived near one another in an apartment complex called the "Frontenac," which contrasted ironically with its namesake in Quebec City, the posh hotel known as Le Chateau Frontenac. Our Frontenac was a set of cockroach-infested transitional apartments where recent immigrants stayed until they could save enough money to afford better living conditions. Our family was one of the last families to leave: we lived there until I was in eighth grade. Even though they were run down and bug-infested, they were a saving grace to me. It was there I had a tightly knit community of Korean immigrant friends who watched out for and helped one another as we struggled together with the hardships of adjusting to our new lives as immigrants. In some ways we attempted to protect one another from the harsh taunts of the kids at school: we were in different grades so the older kids tried to shield the younger ones from the racial slurs of the schoolyard. When we came home, we could play together in a safe environment with children who looked like one another and shared many of the same cultural experiences.

As I reflect on my childhood experiences of racism, I cannot stop thinking about how I am still often viewed as a foreigner by white North American society. It does not matter that I have given up my Korean citizenship and officially become Canadian. To be sure, my perceived foreigner status does not come as a result of my living and working in the United States with a Green Card. I am viewed as such because everyone assumes that Canadians are white or, maybe First Nations, but certainly not Asian—Asians are "foreigners."

Physically, I look different from most persons in my community and I am racially different from those who are white—the group that forms the majority of inhabitants and office holders in my city. I am constantly viewed as a foreigner and am never fully accepted in a society where whiteness sets the standards of how people should look and behave. There are a very few recognizable Asian American female celebrities or other role models in the media or popular culture. TV heroes are (mostly) white males, as are most of the lawyers, doctors, advertising executives, and astute detectives; when other minorities are cast in leading roles, it is almost always someone black or Hispanic, not Asian.

Being a foreigner or being perceived as one is difficult. It means that you are constantly seen as not belonging and thus, easily replaceable. We can become easy targets or scapegoats for things that go wrong in society. We can be mistreated and misrepresented. While the Bible has many stories of foreigners, in most cases, the foreigner is not the "hero," much less someone who is treated as an equal, but someone held with suspicion. Think of how the Bible regards Moses's (non-Israelite) Egyptian heritage in the Old Testament or how the Samaritans as a group are mistreated in the New Testament.

My faith has always been very important to me and I found a lot of peace at church. I grew up in a very conservative Korean Presbyterian Church that catered to Korean immigrants. We spoke to one another in Korean, ate Korean food, and had Korean language and culture lessons. My church, like many others of its kind, did not allow women to be in positions of leadership because of the way it interpreted certain biblical passages in the New Testament about women and authority. So while my church provided me spiritual growth and a retreat from the harsh world, it also forced me to reckon with sexism. Therefore it was both my experiences of racism in the larger society and my experiences of sexism within the church that drove me to study theology and eventually led me to become an ordained minister. While I was able to channel this pain in productive ways, this double bind of racism and sexism has prevented me from feeling completely at home in either the larger society or my ethnic community.

As an adult woman, I have often thought back to my childhood experiences with racism in the broader society and sexism within my own church. I have had to work to heal the pain that shaped me at such a young age. Forming relationships with others, particularly other women of color who have been marginalized in the church for their gender and the broader society for their race-ethnicity, has been especially helpful. While, for the most part, I have come to terms with what happened to me as a young girl, now as a mother I am occasionally brought back to those childhood experiences of hurt, humiliation, and rage when my children encounter racism firsthand (as I will share at the end of this chapter).

Racism and the challenges of being the "perpetual foreigner"

Racism continues to be a problem in North American society and elsewhere. It is a disease that promotes the domination of less powerful and disenfranchised groups by a privileged group in the economic, social, cultural, and intellectual spheres.[1] Racism is so embedded in our society that, like a virus, when federal or state laws ban discrimination on the basis of race, it mutates into more subtle but still harmful forms that are harder to demonstrate in courts. It is thus important to bring racism out from the shadows to reveal it as the anti-Christian institution that it is.

Because of racism, it can be difficult for communities of color to join or be fully accepted within the dominant culture, which then exacerbates their alienation from mainstream society. Even if Asian Americans are touted as the "model minority," many of us still experience an invisible boundary or "glass ceiling." When Nina Davuluri, who is Indian American, became Miss America in 2014, the twitterverse and others on social media exploded with many racist, xenophobic, and ignorant comments about her inability to represent America or about her alleged ties to terrorism or "Muslim extremism" (n.b., Davuluri is darker-skinned and Hindu). To provide another example, while the sports world and nation were enraptured with "linsanity" during NBA player Jeremy Lin's meteoric rise in the 2012 basketball season, he was still racially stereotyped: he was once asked if there was any connection between him and the caricatured and speech-impaired Mr. Yunioshi (played by Mickey Rooney) in the movie "Breakfast at Tiffany's"; ESPN twice ran a "chink in the armor" headline when his team lost their multi-game winning streak; and his success continued to be linked to "Chinese" food (e.g., his photo was commonly superimposed on a fortune cookie—the ice-cream company Ben & Jerry's issued a limited-release "Taste the lin-sanity" frozen yogurt featuring lychee honey swirls and fortune cookies).

If it is difficult for high-profile, successful Asian Americans to be accepted, not exoticized, imagine how much more difficult it is for so many other "ordinary" people of Asian descent who experience racial micro-aggressions on a regular basis. While a wide variety of immigrants from Europe and elsewhere have been able to "melt" into the melting pot of white America, and while blacks, though still viewed as "other," do not today generally experience challenges to their "Americaness," Asian Americans are racialized as "perpetual foreigners" wherein our status as true Americans is continually held in jeopardy.

The "perpetual foreigner" stereotype can be explained accordingly. Almost every Asian has been asked at least one, if not multiple times in her life, "Where are you really from?" This loaded question, which I shall call the "really-question," differs from the usual one, "Where are you from?" The "really-question" figuratively and literally ejects the Asian American respondent to Asia because the assumption behind the question, even if the questioner is oblivious to it, is that Asian Americans cannot be "real" Americans. Even if Asian Americans today are descendants of nineteenth-century transcontinental railroad workers or eighteenth-century Civil War veterans, they are still commonly mistaken for new immigrants. In contrast, the (typically) white questioners, even if they are descendants of first or second-generation immigrants, are taken as "true" Americans. Generally, there is no intention of offense, much less malice, on the part of the questioner. Nonetheless, the person asking us the "really-question" can trigger in us all the racial stereotypes we have contended with since birth: foreigner, unassimilable, unAmerican, or, to use the "O" word, "Oriental." Whether intentionally or not, questioners who pose the "really-question" embody the values and ideology of white supremacy.[2]

The determining factor of perceiving another as a foreigner comes down to physical appearance. If one "looks Asian," it does not matter how many years or generations one has lived in the United States, which country one has sworn allegiance to, or whether one can speak English fluently, one is still commonly considered, and mistaken for, a foreigner. This is not because Asians have different foods, cultural practices, religious heritages, or because they can speak multiple languages. Certainly Irish, Italian, Russian, Polish, Swedish, and other immigrants also possessed different foods, cultural and religious practices, and languages when they arrived on American shores but their descendants have been absorbed into the narratives and identities of North America. In fact, some ethnic groups who were not traditionally understood to be white became white—for example, the Irish—thus showing the historical fluidity of racial categories and constructions of American identity.

But despite the fact that Asian immigrants have been an important part of building the United States and Canada (e.g., consider Chinese American contributions to the transcontinental railroad, Japanese American agricultural contributions in the Western United States, and contemporary Indian American contributions in STEM fields), the fact that Asians look "different" from those considered members of the dominant culture prevents many people from ever recognizing that we belong here just as much as any other immigrant community. In practical terms, this means that fourth or fifth-generation Chinese, Japanese, or Filipino Americans will continue to be lumped together with more recent Asian immigrants and treated as foreign even if they have never had any home or political allegiance except the United States or Canada. Insofar as Asian Americans continue to give birth to children that look distinctively "Asian" (i.e., "Asian" features are not blended with those of other races in interracial marriages or partnerships or they are not surgically altered in ways that minimize their distinctive racial-ethnic features), their physical appearance will set them apart as "foreign."

Marginality and living "betwixt and between"

Racism erodes society and leads to marginalization.[3] Marginalized people live and function in between places. Like many 1.5- or second-generation Asian Americans, I as a Korean American woman neither belong fully to my native (Korean) culture, nor to my host (North American) culture. I was raised to appreciate two sets of values and practices that are complementary in some cases and clashing in others. For instance, in some cases the patriarchal elements of mainstream society "collude" with my East Asian heritage to seek to keep me subservient to male leadership in the home and in the church. I experience these patriarchal pressures in various ways; for example, in being valued by my ethnic community for producing male (but not female) children or not having my ordained clergy status fully respected in Korean church contexts (e.g., women are not always seen as suitable leaders over male deacons and elders and even when we are ordained, we are often relegated to the children's ministry).[4] In other cases, norms of mainstream society clash with those of my ethnic community, such as when the former esteems autonomous decision-making and direct communication or confrontation in ways that the latter does not. Thus in dwelling in two places while belonging to neither one nor the other, neither the ethnic "ghetto" nor mainstream society can serve as a true haven for me.

Asian Americans like me live in a perplexing world as they can be estranged from the majority Anglo American population and other ethnic groups for being "too Asian," and potentially also from other Asians for being "too Americanized" or cut off from their cultural roots (particularly when they are 1.5 or later generations or if they are Asian adoptees to white parents).[5] This double marginalization and non-acceptance has left many Asian Americans not knowing where exactly they belong. For women it is even more complex: they have to endure both the patriarchal attitudes of their Asian ethnicity and their North American context.[6] This is an ongoing problem that needs to be addressed as we engage in life with people from all parts of the world here in North America.

My daughter's encounter with racism

In 2004, I moved to the United States for a new teaching position at a seminary. Later in the fall, my family and I were shopping for a clothes dryer at Sears. While walking around in the department store, three Sears employees walked passed my kids and me. Then to my utter horror, one of them said the brutally degrading *"ching chong, ching chong"* taunt to my then three-year-old daughter.

I was immediately flooded with deeply painful childhood memories: memories of the schoolyard where kids were trying to figure out who I was, kids during recess making those stereotypical clanging chatter noises. For what seemed like an eternity, these memories descended upon me as I stood aghast in that Sears department store.

Somehow I had become resigned to other people thinking of me as a foreigner, but I couldn't allow it in the case of my own children. It was deeply disturbing and alarming. When I witnessed someone treating my daughter as a foreigner, I boiled with rage. How can a child born in this continent still be viewed as a foreigner? This just does not make any sense.

I approached the three men working at Sears and asked them why they said that to my daughter. They laughed about it and said that they didn't mean any harm. They had just returned from a Chinese restaurant and thought that their racial taunts of my daughter were all in fun—just a bit of teasing. I was furious with their response and was distraught for days. I called the Sears manager and complained that their behavior was unacceptable. The manager apologized to me and promised me that those employees would be reprimanded for their behavior. His response neither eliminated my anger, nor eased my deep-seated frustration of knowing that my children were victims of racism and that their generation will continue to be viewed as foreign.

Given the increasingly global nature of our world, I still couldn't believe why my children, and my future grandchildren, would continue to be perceived as foreigners in North America. So how can we work toward a society which will be more welcoming and embracing of all people so that we can work toward perceiving others as equally welcomed and part of God's reign? The solution to the problem of racism can't be to treat Asian Americans as "honorary whites" (instead of as "perpetual foreigners") as some have imagined, because doing so would simply perpetuate the racial hierarchy of whites on top and blacks on bottom and Asians and other communities of color somewhere in between.

Community as refuge

With all the difficulties and problems that I as an Asian American women experience—racism, perpetual foreignness, patriarchy, and marginality—the question remains how we Asian American women can survive and thrive? As people of faith seeking the reign of God, it has been a journey to discover and co-create ways of being that lead to flourishing.

Many Asian American women like me seek to construct our own communities of empowerment. It is these small communities that we have created and built that sustain and restore us. These small communities are distinct from both the dominant Western society and the broader Asian American community. They are a hybrid, a mixing of two or more things with the end result of something new or something different, of their multiple identities and belongings. In these hybrid communities, Asian American women are neither pressured to be more "Westernized," nor assimilated into the dominant community like the "melting pot image," nor forced to remain within the ghettoized areas of society. Rather we form these hybrid communities so that we can learn to accept ourselves and one another as a bi- (or even multi-) cultural and liminal people with our own distinctive gifts, identities, and talents. We celebrate our differences, we support one another, and we share our struggles together, which enriches our communities and allows them to grow and flourish. We are like a "grown-up" version of the ring of childhood friends I had in Le Frontenac apartments in those early years in Canada.

This hybrid community is a semblance of the reign of God. The hybridity of multiple identities and the acceptance and embrace of such identities is what it means to be a part of the body of Christ. Each part of the hybrid community is valued and needed and all the small parts add up to make a beautiful whole. A hybrid community becomes a refuge for Asian American women to seek freedom from racism, marginality, perpetual foreignness, and patriarchy.

Conclusion

Today's context is a world in flux. People are continuously migrating for jobs, for reasons of political or economic instability, or for otherwise better living conditions. As we continue to live in such a complex world, how we view those who are different from us becomes of paramount importance. Will we view them as foreigners or as the "perpetual foreigner"? Or as fellow human beings? Or as fellow countrymen or women? Or as even potential new friends?

We need to be welcoming of those who are different from us and who look different from us. We need to "accept otherness, both within and without . . . with the equanimity born of acceptance of personal and cultural self-division," and thus to meet strangers likewise with equanimity and generosity.[7] As a world that seeks peace, harmony, and love, we need to accept, embrace, and welcome those who are different, to the point where those differences become either invisible or a reason for celebration. For as Gal. 3:28 says, "There is no longer Jew or Greek, there is no longer slave or free, there is no longer male and female; for all of you are one in Christ Jesus."

Notes

1 Fumitaka Matsuoka, *The Color of Faith: Building Community in a Multiracial Society* (Cleveland: United Church Press, 1998), 3.

2 Joseph Cheah, *Race and Religion in American Buddhism* (Oxford: Oxford University Press, 2011), 132.

3 For more on this theme, see Grace Ji-Sun Kim, *Embracing the Other: The Transformative Spirit of Love* (Grand Rapids, MI: Eerdmans, 2015).

4 For more discussion and statistics of women in church leadership, please see Pyong Gap Min, "Severe Underrepresentation of Women in Church Leadership in the Korean Immigrant Community in the United States," *Journal for the Scientific Study of Religion* 47.2 (2008): 225–41.

5 Peter Phan, *Journey at the Margins: Toward an Autobiographical Theology in American-Asian Perspective,* edited by Peter C. Phan and Jung Young Lee (Collegeville, MN: The Liturgical Press, 1999), xix.

6 Gale A. Yee, "Where Are You Really From? An Asian American Feminist Biblical Scholar Reflects on Her Guild," in *New Feminist Christianity: Many Voices, Many Views,* edited by Mary E. Hunt and Diann L. Neu (Woodstock: Skylight Paths, 2010), 79.

7 Harold C. Washington, "Israel's Holy Seed and the Foreign Women of Ezra-Nehemiah: A Kristevan Reading," *Biblical Interpretation* 11.3/4 (2003): 437.

Litany:

Leader: In a world of difference
    Response: Help us learn to cherish diversity
Leader: In a world where we are all sojourners
    Response: Remind us to welcome the stranger
Leader: In a world of complexity
    Response: Challenge us not to simplify
Leader: In a world of noise and chaos
    Response: Teach us to slow down and listen to others
Leader: In a world of hostility and political chaos
    Response: Lead us toward respect and peace with justice

All: Spirit of the Living God, open our hearts and our minds in ways that enable us to build community across lines of difference and learn how to live together in communities of solidarity and support.

Questions for discussion

1   Have you ever been discriminated against because of your race? Do you make or commonly laugh at racist jokes, or at jokes with racial content or that trade on racial stereotypes? How do Grace's experiences of pain allow you to think differently about them?

2   Much of the racism that Grace has endured has been tied to the real or perceived status of Asian Americans in North America as "foreign." She also speaks of the micro-aggression involved when people question where Asians in America "really" come from. Were you born in the place you are now living and if not, do you have experiences of being treated differently, whether positively or negatively, because of it? If so, how have you interacted with "outsiders," immigrants, or other (real or perceived) foreigners?

3   Grace speaks of the comfort she has drawn in the alternative communities of like-minded hybrid and marginalized peoples of which she has been a part. Are you

part of any sub-cultures or alternative communities? If so, what role have they played in your life?

4 Grace's chapter invites readers to ask the following basic question of humanity: How do we welcome the stranger within us? How do we embrace those who are different from ourselves?

Suggestions for further reading

Brock, Rita Nakashima, Jung Ha Kim, Kwok Pui-lan, and Seung Ai Yang, eds. *Off the Menu: Asian and Asian North American Women's Religion and Theology*. Louisville, KY: Westminster John Knox Press, 2007.

Hong, Christine J. *Identity, Youth, and Gender in the Korean American Church*. New York, NY: Palgrave Pivot, 2015.

Pak, Su Yon, Unzu Lee, Jung Ha Kim, and Myung Ji Cho. *Singing the Lord's Song in a New Land: Korean American Practices of Faith*. Louisville, KY: Westminster John Knox Press, 2005.

6

Re-membering rape
(sexual assault)

Marcia Mount Shoop

Descending

an underneath
dug by fingernails
quietly at night
carefully in broad day light
and consistently through time

deep slow calm
and sometimes dark
when it needs to be
reach and feel the confines
of a world small enough
to be safe

loving you
untenable
so there it is a
cosmic truth
a fragrance and angels dancing
inside eye lids closed
imagine

periodically there is a crowd
peering in
sometimes gawking and taunting
fade into a crevice
ease into shadowy entrails
they will tire of no movement
and pursue a more
active specimen

the crowd can be majestic
strong dancing ones
who know the medicine I need
stretch into some long
left-alone anteroom

sometimes they are small
needing me, calling me
shrieking
or laughing but wanting me to come and see
come here and see

* * *

The email from my sister was a simple suggestion. "Thought
you might be interested." It was a study they were doing at the
University about the connection between previous sexual trauma
and the severity of premenstrual syndrome symptoms for women.
The first time she sent it, I disregarded it. I made no immediate
decision one way or another. I simply did not respond.

I had few thoughts before moving on to open my next email.
Maybe I should participate. Maybe I was ready. I also felt a low-
grade kind of invasion, dismissal, and misunderstanding from my
sister making this suggestion this way. But I moved on until I got
another email a few weeks later. This time it was a friendly reminder
from that same sister. "It looks like they still need people for this
study. Thought you might be interested."

That's when the old script kicked in for me—so smoothly that I
didn't even notice. I needed to make that phone call to be responsible,
to allow for some redemptive possibility to emerge from my rape.
Never mind the fact that I have written a book about it, traveled
around and talked about it, and ministered to many who shared the

experience.[1] Never mind all that. None of that counted now. This invitation, to take part in this scientific study, was what I needed to do now to "do the right thing."

So, I called. I waited for the person doing the questionnaire for the study to call me back. The person on the original phone call explained that this person would call me to take an inventory of my experience to see if I qualified for the study. I felt nervous waiting. Would I qualify? What would she want to know? Strangely, I thanked her when I picked up the phone on her call back. What was I thanking her for?

She proceeded to ask me lots of questions about what kinds of PMS symptoms I have. She asked about my rape and the aftermath. "How old were you?" "Are your periods heavy?" "Do you ever feel like you will die young?"

I answered the questions clearly, responsibly, and in a controlled, matter-of-fact tone. I felt vacant. My legs started to itch. I was going to someplace else, some place where this wasn't really happening to me, where I was going through the motions but was not really there.

The sensation of vacating my body usually starts in my toes and goes up subtly snaking itself through my soul. I go to a space aloof from the goings on. I watch. I wait. I hold my breath.

I don't really remember what the woman said next. I think it was something like "I will talk this over with my supervisor and I will get back to you about when you can get started. You'll need to wait for your next period and then come in after that." "Ok," I said, "Thank you."

I hung up and went on with my work with the shaky kind of feeling you have when you've just had a heart-stopping experience—a near miss on the highway, a startle from someone coming up behind you who you didn't know was there. I felt weak, foggy. I took note of my condition only to resolve to try and ignore it. Everything was fine. I am a responsible adult in her forties and my participation in this study is a good thing for me to do at this point in my life.

Even with everything I know and have written about PTSD, even after living with the embodied marks of sexual trauma for thirty some years, even though I had descended back into that place before, I was unprepared for the horrible spiral I went into after this phone call. With no ability to stop the vortex of return to my past,

I found myself in an arrested space for days. I couldn't be touched. I couldn't sleep. The old voice that told me it was my fault, that I was lying, that he was going to kill me if I told anyone began its continuous looping playback.

And I moved through this demoralizing trip into the sensations and sadness of my rape and abuse while recognizing the familiar stages and steps along the way. I emerged a few days later with a new clarity. I would not, I could not participate in the study.

It was a relief that I reached a voice mail when I called back. "I won't be able to participate in the study. Thank you for your time. I will be interested to hear your findings." I hung up thinking I could save them the trouble.

* * *

I re-member rape every day. From my thoughts to my muscle twitches, I re-member rape by its effects. I re-member rape through sensations and stories of bodies ravaged and regenerating.

Sexual violence is not a once-and-for-all occurrence for those whose lives it invades. The deep, cellular effects ripple out into bodies, generations, family systems, institutions, and communities. Even with all the years that stretch out between the fifteen-year-old girl I was when I was raped and the woman in her forties that I am today, I continue to live with the deeply entrenched habits of my body that took hold in me so long ago.

Some sensations can only be expressed in movement or stillness. Washes of sadness, panic, fear, and isolation move through me with periodic rhythms that are hard to predict, but sometimes effortlessly triggered. Ubiquitous violence finds a home in me when I meet others who have also survived—tragic connective tissue that defies the isolation that accompanies rape. Somehow my own experience of violence, survival, and healing are a portal for others who cannot or do not or never did speak.

Re-membering rape is embodied testimony to the power of bodies to hold and to heal the pain of living in a violent world. The Incarnation, what Julian of Norwich called the "one-ing" of Divinity and humanity that Christianity particularly locates in the Christ event, gives me a template for such truth about bodies: a body made like mine, a body punctured by violence, and a body resurrected by Divine defiance of human cruelty. My own body finds redemption in Christ's body digesting a way to live within mine, a way to come back from repeated returns to the brink. The Incarnation knits through me the simultaneity of life and death.[2]

The shadows and contours of living with rape tell this truth over and over again: redemption is no final victory. Nor is redemption simply survival. Redemption courses through the blood in my veins, it animates the cells dividing within the recesses of how I am made. Redemption is nerve endings regenerating, synapses spidering their way to an adapted way of staying engaged.

Surfacing

He was there
 in darkness, tender, knowing
The tears of loneliness, despair
 they went—washed, flowing into His hand
From my face to His hand
 there was no nothingness
 but a symmetry
 a seeing one,
 that knowing.
What happened pouring into His hand from my tears
 transformed from wastewater
 to the threads of harm
 I needed someone to know firsthand.
Nakedness consecrated
 I know now.
 All those years
 I felt that hand on my face
 and longed for a corollary instinct to see me.
One day I took his hand, finally
 when the pain was back,
 fresh as the day it was born—on that day of quiet violence,
 I took his hand and put it there
Letting the cells of memory tell their truth.
Tears—
 went, washed, finding flesh
Warm fullness and glows of ethereal light
Re-membered that He was there
  still.

Trauma seeps into cracks and crevices beyond our conscious reach. It penetrates systems and sources. It distorts time and space. Trauma is not linear. It is not neat and tidy. It blurs boundaries and elides our patterns of memory. Descending back into its shadows periodically is a part of my life. I've had to accept that. And as I notice its chaotic patterns and embodied effects I am more and more able to receive the wisdom, the symmetry that surfaces also in unruly emergence. I have learned to recognize the generosity in the bubbling up of awareness along with the grief of what can never be repaired.

* * *

Trying to put my rape in the past combusted with a simple night at the movies during the first few months of my marriage in my mid-twenties. *Dead Man Walking*, the movie with Sean Penn and Susan Sarandon, had a scene with a young woman's naked body in a field being assaulted. The movie watcher had an aerial view. That bird's eye view, the view I had had when I left my body being assaulted, must have been the key that opened up a horrible doorway that I had tried to lock. I had no conscious memory of my disassociations at the time, yet the visual trigger was potent enough to set off a stream of nightmares that kept me from sleeping for weeks. The nightly reliving of being raped took over. It was the "life interruption" the books tell you about with PTSD.

I couldn't sleep. Newly married, I could not engage in sexual intercourse. My mind raced. My body clenched. I bled. I just couldn't do it. I felt an immense amount of guilt about that. My husband was respectful, loving, and patient. I did not want to hurt him with this thing from my past. I tried to fight through, tried to move on. I was ashamed that I couldn't shake off the past and be someone who was fine, over it, healthy, happy.

One of my sisters told me to call the Rape Crisis Center when I told her about the nightmares. Mary T. is the therapist who answered my phone call. I told her it wasn't really an emergency since it happened so many years ago. I told her someone else told me I should call. After hearing a few more sentences of what was going on for me she told me to come in right away. For several months she listened, named, affirmed, and encouraged me. She gave me permission to grieve and to find words for truth-telling to myself, to my husband, to my family. I began to claim this story as mine and accept that it would be my story forever.

Rom. 8:28 had always been a favorite Bible passage of mine growing up. "We know that all things work together for good for those who love God, who are called according to his purpose." Once I started to really deal with the sexual violence of my teenage years, this passage became anger inducing. God could *not* use all things to the good. Being raped was not good, nothing about it was. Redemption, the linear, cause and effect kind, became repulsive to me. My repeated return through sexual trauma made redemption something I desperately needed to taste even as it became a lie I could no longer swallow.

* * *

Living with trauma has stretched me into theologically neglected spaces. I have to find my way back to being at home in my own body again and again. Incarnation has room for trauma to show itself, to be witnessed to, to testify.[3] How has Jesus saved my life? The Jesus who was there with me through it all wasn't sin-obsessed. He was honest, he was powerfully compassionate. His presence kept me alive. He told me he understood, and he knew what really happened.

Atonement calculus loops through sin, guilt, and forgiveness with different metaphors for human need and Divine accomplishment. When I use the term "atonement" I am referring to the traditional Christian teaching that Jesus's death on the cross saved humanity from our sinful condition in some ultimate way. There have been numerous interpretations of that dynamic in the history of Christian theology and dogmatics. But even with this diversity of interpretation in the tradition, these theories share a common denominator in the centrality of the cross for the accomplishment of redemption.[4] Jesus's suffering and death solve a problem for humanity and finalize a salvific accomplishment on our behalf. The atonement is supposed to mean that the world is different now. Only, in my experience, it's not.[5]

The Jesus who "died for my sins" does not resonate with the Jesus who came to me in my trials. Jesus bore the weight of sin and suffering on the cross, but not in a way that tidied it up. Jesus lived and died enmeshed in suffering, the same suffering that I know. And not just that, but Jesus lives for my flourishing, for ours. This Christ-vitality does not erase suffering, nor does this Christ-vitality inhabit suffering with a promise of future redemption, justice, and resolution. It is Divine vulnerability that saves us and generates the unique power God has to keep stitching redemptive threads through it all.

Dwelling

I am the vine, you are the branches.
Those who abide in me and I in them bear much fruit,
because apart from me you can do nothing . . .
I have said these things to you so that my joy may be in you,
and that your joy may be complete. (Jn 15:5, 11)

We live in the distortions intertwined in our bodies through life in a world where harm and suffering are a part of the deal. And stitched into the mode and mechanism of our experience is a shimmering capacity to regenerate, to grow new shoots where one cut off withers.

* * *

She asked me what I needed. I needed to run away. I needed to move my legs, to get away. She took my feet near my ankles in her hands and quickly moved them up and down like I was running. Tears came in streams, not drops. All those years of running, the sensation of numbness in my legs, the scabs from itching my calves into being there, and the hollowness I had learned only recently to recognize in the whole lower half of my body—all of these wise and tragic ways my body tells my story stitched their way into a fleeting wash of redemption—a ghostly catharsis, that swept into my flexed muscles and tensed up lungs. And the fluttering rush of coming back home into my body became something I could recognize and claim. I befriended this new redemptive rhythm I could invite and embrace. It felt like resurrection—electric, soothing, my own carnal knowledge of some Divine spark that had bided its time for this moment.

* * *

Redemption is such embodied connection—that my nerve endings have rejuvenated enough to feel with immediacy what I can't think my way through. The subtlety and power of such an intricate power to transform is stunning. To live trusting such an excruciating and regenerating rhythm is a primal path etched along eons of sentient life. This redemptive creek bed flows through us and invites us to surrender to its promise of connection and regeneration.

The Incarnation, God dwelling among us, delivers us from the snares of dualism,[6] rigid orthodoxy, shame, and blame. Jesus embodies the Divine capacity to inhabit competing needs with generosity, provision, wisdom, and love. Eternity is not a reward for righteousness or a destination, but an ontological truth about who we are and how we are made. It is the Divine spark in us, the *imago Dei* that is ours that connects us to the unending thread of life. The Incarnation tells us who we are and calls us back to ourselves, to each other, and to God again and again.

* * *

I've learned now to be prepared. When I go and speak about rape to any group, there is always at least one person who emerges from that event to tell me her or his secret.

"That happened to me."

"It was a long time ago."

"I've never told anyone this."

"I try not to think about it."

"No one really acknowledged what happened."

"We just acted like it was over and done with."

And for a few days after, other voices will emerge. A phone call. An email. A person I meet at some other event, even people who were not at the event where I spoke about the rape. It is as if a passage way opens and more people step into the transition from silence to story. I dream dreams of grief and betrayal. I feel heavy with the hidden tears and scars of generations from across time and space. I cry tears on their behalf and breathe into this collective chasm of violence. There is a symmetry to it that is tender and potent—it is not just mine, but a shared world that I occupy—called into audibility and connection. I can only hold my place there for a while. Then I need rest, because I know I will be back there again and hear, see, feel the tangle of shared harm.

* * *

How we abide there with our own truth and our deep connection to others embodies the choices we all make between lives of triviality and lives of zest. And the decision to "be there" shifts us toward a more robust embodied existence with all the delight, anguish, restlessness, and redemption it entails. "The incarnation is the unspeakable joyousness that we dwell in at the intersection of Divinity and humanity."[7] It is that joy which creates the conditions for re-membering rape to be life-giving, even to the good.

I hold within me peace and unknowing. I dwell in the story my body holds each day with new possibilities. As a wife, I am thankful for intimacy that I enjoy—hard-won, beautiful. And I am thankful for a partner who knows and honors me in ways that still startle me sometimes. As a mother, I choose truth-telling with my children about what happened to me. They need to know, and I need to allow the story to unfold for them as they are able to receive it. It is clear to me that they already hold it within themselves in different ways. Their lives are already tangled up in the harm and the healing. I am a different mother than I would have been. Especially when an undeserved flash of anger is directed toward them, I grieve how the sharp edges can cut them.

Just as I could not erase the memories of weight bearing down on me, I also cannot extract the exaggerated responses to certain situations I encounter with my children. My blood runs cold when my elementary school–aged daughter tells me a boy wants to kiss her at school. I want her to know herself and be able to anticipate trouble. I pray for ways to allow both my son and daughter to come into their own sexual awareness without shame and without being blindsided by the way our bodies can be harmed by other bodies. It is an impossible task before me. Dwelling in the redemptive possibilities means honoring my deep connection with my children no matter how their sexual awakening unfolds.

Re-membering rape can regenerate more than brutalized bodies—this regeneration weaves its vitality through all bodies who live, breathe, suffer, love, and yearn for compassion. Descending, surfacing, and dwelling continue to move and breathe my life into its own. And the compassionate witness, the One who knows, continues to abide. Even now, the work of writing this chapter hastens me to the underneath, to the sensations of loss and of regeneration. And I breathe a strong ocean wind. I see an osprey move over the waters looking for food, swooping into tumultuous water and coming up with some new sustenance to share.

Notes

1 Marcia Mount Shoop, *Let the Bones Dance: Embodiment and the Body of Christ*, Louisville, KY: Westminster John Knox Press, 2010.

2 See Victoria Rue's reflections on death and dying in this volume for a different treatment of the Incarnation (Chapter 9).

3 Shelly Rambo asserts that this "discourse about traumatic suffering must extend beyond the cross to the middle territory of survival." Shelly Rambo, *Spirit and Trauma: A Theology of Remaining* (Louisville, KY: Westminster John Knox Press, 2010), 157.

4 These traditional interpretations of atonement include ransom theories, satisfaction theories, exemplar theories, and substitutionary theories.

5 Delores S. Williams uses her "ministerial vision" to take the emphasis away from the cross, toward the life of Christ. For Williams the Incarnation embodies itself in whoever helps us survive and improve the quality of our lives in our everydayness. With her "survival/quality-of-life" hermeneutics she explains that God does not always liberate, but that God gives us survival skills and points us toward resources to help us survive. Delores S. Williams, *Sisters in the Wilderness: The Challenge of Womanist God-Talk* (Maryknoll, NY: Orbis Books, 1993).

6 An expression of dualism in Christianity, particularly in Christianity's Western theological tradition, is the need to draw hard lines between things like flesh and Spirit, God and humanity, body and soul. This dualistic tendency also deeply informs our Western scientific heritage about splits between mind and body, rationality and emotion.

7 Wendy Farley, *Gathering Those Driven Away: A Theology of Incarnation* (Louisville, KY: Westminster John Knox Press, 2011), 14.

Re-membering Eucharist:
A ritual exploration

Church teachings around who is authorized to "do" the Eucharist vary across denominations. While some readers may feel the space to celebrate Eucharist in an official capacity and space, others may feel less room for that to be possible. May this ritual be an invitation to explore how table fellowship can take on a Eucharistic character even outside authorized liturgical spaces and language. While your ritual exploration may or may not qualify as an official celebration of Eucharist, your encounter around the table can be space for practicing beloved community that bears the marks of Eucharistic community (practices of truth-telling, embodied healing, connecting, redemption, etc.).

Invitation: Find your way to the table set by Holy Mystery, by the Holy One who calls to you in your deepest need and in your greatest gifts. From East and West, from North and South, from work and rest, from loneliness and crowdedness, come. This is the gathering space, the place for broken bodies, for dis-membered ones, for the betrayed, the ignored, the complacent, the wronged, the guilty, the innocent. There is a place for you. There is plenty for you. This is a place where you get what you need and there is enough. This is a table of justice, mercy, and healing community.

Great Thanksgiving:

- Invite those gathered for Eucharist/table fellowship to pray together in some way that makes space for shared power, for vulnerability, for silence, and for connection.

- Invite people to turn to the person next to them and share something they are thankful for with each other. Come back to the full circle and have each person share the thanksgiving from the person with whom they talked. Have them share that thanksgiving on behalf of the person, using their name in the sharing. OR

- Make space for people to voice prayers aloud for creation, for forgiveness, for thanksgiving, for others, for the beloved community. OR

- Use the Loud Prayer, taught by Welsh Missionaries to communities in Korea and parts of Africa. The Loud Prayer was used to revitalize the church. Everyone prays as loud as they can for whatever the Spirit moves them to pray for at the same time. The prayer ends when it ends, when the gathered community feels it end.

- In Christian contexts you can end the prayer with a unison Lord's Prayer, invite those people to pray that prayer in the language of their hearts whatever that may be for each person gathered.

Words of Institution: When beloved communities gather, hungry for redemption and healing and connection, we recall the stories that remind us who we are. Christian scripture tells us about a night when so much hung in the balance. It was the night of his arrest that he and his friends went to an upstairs room. There must have been tension, anticipation, heaviness, confusion, and love in that room. Jesus wanted to spend some time with his friends eating and praying with them, blessing them, looking them in the eye and telling them the truth about who they were and who they could become.

The story passed down tells us that Jesus took bread that night and blessed it and broke it. He said, "This is my body, broken for you. Take. Eat." We do this re-membering Him.

In the same way he took the cup and said "This cup is the new covenant sealed in my blood, poured out for you. Drink it, all of you." We do this re-membering Him.

When we eat this bread and drink this cup together. We show forth, we re-member, we embody the transforming birth, life, death, and resurrection of Jesus Christ. He abides in us and we in Him. The vine, the branches, bearing fruit.

Communion of the People: Share the elements using intinction, a method of serving communion that shares a common cup into which the gathered community dips their bread. Face one another; bless one another with words—the bread of life, the cup of salvation. You may want to have someone also providing a body blessing, anointing each person with oil before or after communion is received. It was a gift to people with food allergies to have the same bread served to all, instead of separate stations. (Remember people with Celiac Disease cannot dip in a cup that has had bread that contains wheat dipped in it.)

Prayer after Communion: In your mystery, Holy One, you fill us with bread and the fruit of the vine even as you fill us with your presence and your unique power to redeem, to transform. You have taken a dis-membered Body, a Body with parts cast away, ignored, harmed, diminished and knit us together, re-membered us. May this nourishment awaken us to our identity and our healing capacity in this broken and beautiful world.

Extending the Table: If there is leftover bread, share it around the circle again and encourage everyone to use the leftovers for a life-giving purpose: people can share a piece with a friend, family member, or stranger. Take some of the leftovers and feed the birds or a pet you love. Or maybe someone at the table needs more for themselves. Leftover juice/wine should also be used for a life-giving purpose—hydrating something that is alive and that benefits from that kind of liquid (grape juice or wine).

Questions for discussion

1 This chapter addresses the pain of living in a violent world. Where do you feel this pain? Where and how does your family and your community experience the world's violence? Where do you find support and healing?

2 Marcia describes her own struggles with traditional theological ideas about incarnation, redemption, and atonement. What theological questions do you wrestle with about the nature of salvation and redemption? How does Marcia's discussion and reimagining of these traditional theological concepts speak to your understanding of God or of what it means to be human? How and why does the central insight of incarnational theology—that God became flesh in the person and body of Jesus Christ—matter to you?

3 We often carry the memories of trauma in our bodies. What did you think about/feel as you read Marcia's description of living with trauma? What are some other kinds of loss that connected to this description?

4 Marcia writes about the "responsibility" she felt to have something redemptive come out of her experience of being raped—for example, by participating in studies, talking and publishing about it, and participating in others'

healing process. What are some ways you can describe the relationship between trauma and redemption? What does healing mean to you in the context of the faith?

Suggestions for further reading

Jones, Serene. *Trauma and Grace: Theology in a Ruptured World.* Louisville, KY: Westminster John Knox Press, 2009.

Parker, Rebecca Ann, and Rita Nakashima Brock. *Saving Paradise: How Christianity Traded Love of This World for Crucifixion and Empire.* Boston: Beacon Press, 2009.

West, Traci C. *Wounds of the Spirit: Black Women, Violence, and Resistance Ethics.* New York: New York University Press, 1999.

7

Girl-talk
(gossip)

Elizabeth Hinson-Hasty

Saturday morning, 5:30 a.m.—I roll out of bed, take off my pajamas, pull on my sweats, and put on my walking shoes. After quickly finger brushing my hair, I twist it up in a bun and secure it with a barrette. I make my way downstairs as quietly as possible so I won't wake up the dog or other members of my family.

5:40 a.m.—My first stop is the coffee pot. I experience a rush of inner joy when seeing that the automatic timer setting worked. Coffee is dripping into the pot and nearly ready to be consumed. Twenty minutes now to savor a cup or two as I prepare myself for a weekly pleasure—an hour-and-a-half escape from the daily grind. On Saturdays, I regularly schedule a six-mile walk with my friend, Chloe.

5:50 a.m.—The vibration of my cell phone on a side table by the sofa lets me know that a text message has arrived: "Leaving my driveway. May be five minutes late." I chuckle to myself as I wonder when the term "late" could be associated with a 6:00 a.m. walk on Saturday morning, but every second counts in our worlds.

Both Chloe and I are mothers of two children and have some responsibilities of caring for other members of our extended families, including our aging parents. She works full-time at home. I work full-time as a university professor. We are definitely feeling the pressure of being the sandwich generation. Time cannot go unnoticed. There is never enough of it. We squeeze in minutes to exercise on a daily basis, but, I must admit, the main focus of this weekly event is not the walk; it is the space and time to talk.

6:05 a.m.—I see the headlights from her car glint on the living room window as she turns into my driveway. I bolt out of the front door. For the next six miles, we are walking and have precisely ninety minutes to devote to talking.

So, the truth is out: I am a talker. I talk problems out on the pavement and tend to make important decisions in consultation with others, both family and friends. It is no secret that women are commonly stereotyped as "talkers." But I wonder if we always understand what is happening in women's conversations and why they are so often cast in a negative light.

Conversations among women are frequently dismissed as "gossip" and stigmatized through the use of derogatory terms like "chatty women" who are "talking behind someone's back," engaging in "idle talk," or "feeding the rumor mill." When women get together to talk, we are often accused of "gossiping" and the implication is clear—to be a "gossip" implies, at best, idleness and meddling, at worst, injury and ill-will. Can you think of any popular images of gossips in the media who are men? None come to my mind. We commonly refer to men's conversations as "hanging out" or "networking." However, we now know that men engage in gossip just about as much as women. Some sociological psychologists think men gossip even more![1] Nonetheless, women remain the brunt of jokes about gossip in US culture.

Church women have become particularly associated with negative or destructive forms of gossip in US culture. The prayer chain is sometimes equated with the gossip chain. Many of you may remember comedian Dana Carvey's famous skit called "Church Chat" on *Saturday Night Live* where he dressed up as a little old church lady named Enid Strict. Wearing drab and dowdy clothes, Strict personified all the stereotypes of pious, "gossipy," and judgmental church ladies who evaluate the moral failures of others, particularly other women. Strict let the punch line of "Church Chat" slip out of her mouth as her face displayed a sense of Machiavellian pleasure while speculating about the cause of the moral turpitude of women—"Could it be Satan?" Comedic interpretations of women as gossipers mask the role that religious, particularly Christian, traditions have played in influencing the way we think about women's conversations and how women pass along moral wisdom.

The term "gossip" has not always been used as an epithet/insult. Its origins in the Middle Ages bear witness to the important social role women's shared speech can play in developing community, offering support and nurture to women friends and family members, and ensuring care for the vulnerable. I want to claim the definition of gossip that stereotypes of women obscure—the concept of gossip as "God-sib" as it originated in the Middle Ages. Originally, the watchful attention of a God-sib was not offered in a spirit of judgment, but rather with the intention of expressing feelings about the importance of the actions and experiences of others to us and to God. My experience of friendship and freedom found in conversations with other women tells me that constructive gossip creates strong social bonds, serves as a way of sharing knowledge and enlarging social networks, enables women to discern in community what we value most, and provides a means of passing along practical moral wisdom.

Gossips as "God-sibs"

The term "gossip" in English first emerged in the Middle Ages with reference to the role that godparents, known as "God-sibs," played in two important rituals after the birth of a child: baptism and churching (the reintegration of women into the community after childbirth). Gossip came to refer to the conversations of those, primarily women, who gathered together before or after the enactment of those rituals.

At that time, rituals in the church specifically related to women's experiences also involved their families and children. Infants were ordinarily baptized quickly after birth, which meant that mothers, who were recovering from labor and delivery, could not be present for this sacrament. The midwife who assisted in the mother's labor carried the child to the church and sometimes served as a godparent. Godparents sponsored, shared the name of, and even received the child from the priest after baptism. Their role as "God-sibs" was to be spiritual kin and to help the child develop and grow in her or his life of faith.

Women in the Middle Ages did not have the freedom to choose to leave their homes after giving birth. Medieval church doctrine placed restrictions upon women after childbirth, including barring them from entering the church or from having sex with their husbands. Before a new mother could do these things, she had to participate in another important ritual known as "churching" through which she would be purified.

The origins of churching can be found in two biblical texts: Lev. 12:2-8 and Lk. 2:22-39. The book of Leviticus contains holiness codes, which proscribe that a woman wait for a set number of days (thirty-three days upon birth of a son and sixty-six upon birth of a daughter) before reentering the synagogue on account of her ritual uncleanliness from childbirth. Luke tells the story of Mary reentering the synagogue after performing all purification rites following the birth to Jesus (Lk. 2:22-39). Mary's purification was celebrated as early as the fifth century as the Feast of Candlemas. By the fifteenth century, the ritual was common in many parts of Europe.[2] A woman's churching was conducted only in the presence of a priest or pastor and the other women who had attended to her during the birth. These women also came to be known as "gossips," a term used to describe the socializing that took place after churching.

Imagine the importance of conversation among a woman and her "God-sibs" after the former had given birth, been isolated from others, and remained secluded in the home. This feeling of isolation experienced after giving birth is something many women can still identify with today. To be sure, many women aren't required by religious or cultural restrictions to stay at home after giving birth, though some who are financially able to may choose to do so because of their need and desire to bond with the baby and physically recover from labor and delivery. Both of my children were born in the month of March, very early in the spring. It was too cold to even take a newborn baby outside for a stroll. The prospect of people visiting my home was very exciting to me. My first visitors in both cases were members of my church who brought food and came to greet the baby and hear the story of the birth. I guess we could call them "God-sibs" or gossips. In the best sense, these "God-sibs" were like spiritual guides. They supported and affirmed the value of my life and the life of my children in the community. They went back to the community to share news about the birth, the difficulty of my labor, and baby's health. Their gossip nurtured an awareness that what happened in my home mattered to others and to God as the community of faith was invited to celebrate the new baby and to support, even feed, my family and me as we cared for a new child.

Gossip's fall from grace

So why don't most of us think of gossips in this more positive light as "God-sibs" anymore? The answer involves translation issues in biblical texts and patriarchal norms—phenomena best explained by a larger discussion of how our understanding of talk among women has been shaped by dominant interpretations of Jewish and Christian scripture and traditions.

Derogatory talk or making slanderous comments about another person has traditionally been considered sinful, dangerous, and even evil in some instances in Jewish and Christian teachings. The holiness codes in Leviticus include this teaching: "Do not go up and down as a talebearer ("*rakhil*" in Hebrew) among your people" (Lev. 19:16). Bearing false witness is condemned as "*lashon hara*," a Hebrew term meaning "evil talk" or "evil tongue." "*Lashon hara*" is named in some Talmudic sources as a sin comparable to idolatry, adultery, and murder.

One of the reasons that slander is seen as such a grave sin is because the damage done by malicious comments cannot be undone. Money that is stolen can be repaid, but slandering another person's reputation could have a lifelong impact. In courts of law in the ancient world, a person could be accused of a crime just by two or three eyewitnesses (see Deut. 17:6 and 19:15). The need to tell the truth and not make false accusations was paramount to the well-being of others and to the system of justice as a whole. Rabbi Moses ben Maimon, a Jewish philosopher who lived in the Middle Ages, concluded from his interpretation of Deut. 17:6 and passages in the Talmud that women could not be counted among those qualified to serve as witnesses.[3]

Still, the Babylonian Talmud also includes neutral references to women's talking. One reference to women's talking in the Talmud can be found in Tractate Kiddushin. The Hebrew term used there to refer to women talking is not "*lashon hara*," but "*sicha*," which bears no negative connotations and is used in neutral ways in other places in the Talmud. However, a much later English translation of Talmud from 1944 construes "*sicha*" as gossip: "Ten measures of gossip descended to the world: nine were taken by women."[4] Within the literary context, gossip appears to be given a negative connotation that is not associated with the Hebrew word "*sicha*."

A key text that can help us understand early Christian views of women's talk, more specifically conversations among widows or unmarried women, is found in 1 Tim. 5:13. The author of Timothy was writing to a particular community in Ephesus about widows and their behavior. The Greek word used for widows here, "*chera*," identifies both women who were once married and left vulnerable after the death of their husbands and women who were choosing to renounce marriage and take vows of celibacy. This distinction is important. According to the ethic of the early Christian communities, older widows, who were at risk and financially vulnerable and had previously been part of patriarchal households, should be cared for by community of faith (see 1 Tim. 5:4-16). However, younger women who were choosing to renounce marriage were seen as subversive and thus dangerous. A literal translation from the Greek text of 1 Tim. 5:13 reads, "and at the same time they learned to be idle, going around the houses; and not only idle, but practice nonsense and busy bodies, speaking the things not proper." The concern expressed in 1 Tim. 5:13 appears to be about young women who freed themselves from the constraints placed upon them within the patriarchal household: these women started "meddling" in other people's business. There are some examples where women in the ancient world chose to renounce marriage to become prophetesses!

Throughout the centuries, theologians who contributed to the formation of Western Christian thought shared similar concerns about the perceived idleness of women who were not part of the patriarchal household. Women outside the male control must have had more time on their hands, thus prompting Chrysostom to characterize idleness as the "teacher of every sin." Reformation theologian John Calvin thought "women were prone to talkativeness by nature."[5] Martin Luther interpreted the passage in 1 Timothy to include a sexual element in the behavior of widows: "To feed a young widow, then, is to nourish a serpent in your bosom. They begin to grow wanton and to seek out men with their wanton ways."[6] One problem with these examples from the Christian theological tradition is the limited perspectives of the interpreters.

Classical speculations about what women were really doing when they had time to talk were provided primarily by men during times when they would have been outsiders to women's networks of friends or companions.

The way women's talk is construed and the connotation of the word gossip has evolved since the Middle Ages. An example is found in the way the Greek word *"phlyaroi"* used in 1 Tim. 5:13 has been translated over time. *"Phlyaroi"* literally means "those who practice nonsense,"[7] but is translated as "gossips" in the New Revised Standard Version, Common English Bible, and New American Standard Bible. An earlier translation, the King James Version, opted to use the "tattlers" in this verse. By the time the King James Version was completed in 1611, the term "gossip" had already come into parlance. There are examples of positive references to God-sibs and gossips in popular literature from that era. The godparents of King Henry's daughter Elizabeth are called "noble gossips" in Shakespeare's play Henry VIII. You may find it intriguing that the New King James Version (commissioned in 1975) and KJ21 (described online as an update in the use of language within the original King James bible rather than a translation) both use the term "gossip" rather than "tattlers."

Early on, words like "idle talk" and "jangling" made their way into common speech as gossip began to imply trivial conversation. By the nineteenth century, gossip became primarily associated with slander and malicious talk. Gossip is now considered in contemporary US pop culture to be an "exaggeration or fabrication of a story, regarding somebody other than the tale bearer, in the absence of this person who is being discussed—for the malicious purpose of demeaning, slandering or tarnishing this person's reputation."[8] This definition is a far cry from the talk of "God-sibs."

Gossip as foundational to building community

Gossip is one of the oldest means of sharing information and remains very common. If we are going to reclaim the value of gossip in building community, we need to reject the more recent definition of gossip as malicious and slanderous. Many of us know that gossip is women's talk—it's what we do when we get together and share the stories of our lives with one another and when we talk about our friends, families, and neighbors and their lives and their stories. When we do this out of love and the compassion that we bear for one another, this kind of constructive gossip functions to share moral wisdom, strengthen bonds of friendship and family, and support people who may be struggling under the weight of their burdens.

Sharing intimate details about our lives and the lives of others in the space of conversation among friends is one way we find the courage to tell and face up to the truth and discover reliable support networks. In our culture and other cultures around the world, women are too often required to make moral decisions according to timeframes established by other's needs, standards, and values. Talking together is one of the most important ways that we, as women, determine our *own* courses of action.

Social scientific research within the last twenty-five years invites us to reconsider how gossip functions among women. Some sociologist psychologists estimate that nearly 80 percent of our conversations today include some form of gossip. These studies recognize the ways in which gossip is a part of building "reputational systems," forms "social cohesion," and can be deemed "pro-social" behavior.[9]

Gossip maintains an important truth-telling function in our society. By not sharing intimate details of our lives and of others, women can increase their own social isolation from others and inadvertently maintain the privilege and power for both those who lord it over them and those policies and practices that are unjust. The situation is compounded in situations of abuse, the cycle of abuse involves intimidating a person to control and prevent her from sharing anything that would challenge her abuser's power. Talking about our friends and family members who are hurting themselves, hurting others, or being hurt is thus an incredibly important social task that is born out of love and compassion. When the abusive situation is discovered by women friends or neighbors, they may need to share details about the situation or "gossip" in an effort to determine a course of action and to intervene.

On a communal level, gossip can be equally important in truth-telling about unjust policies or employment practices. One of the situations that comes to my mind is the importance of women who work being able to talk about the way they are paid. I can attest to the fact that when women friends have shared stories about how they were compensated by employers that allowed them to compare their salary with men, they almost always discovered disparities. They also learned what strategies men had used to get higher pay.

Women in wealthier countries share in common with other marginalized people around the world the need to discover safe and reliable ways of navigating potentially dangerous journeys. The lack of sufficient legal avenues for people to immigrate to the United States results in many seeking to cross our southern border taking risky and dangerous paths to cross the highly militarized US border. A sociologist named Joanna Dreby points out that gossip (*"chisme"* in Spanish) in the context of migrant journeys is a means of "obtaining and passing along information to other members of the community" and a "mechanism for influencing others."[10] Gossip, in short, plays a key role in helping migrants find a safe passage to cross the US border. Gossiping about the journey that lies ahead, be it about the difficult terrain or US border defenses, is essential to the traveler's safety and survival. Dreby observes that the "cooperative aspects of gossip are more vital to shaping women's migration patterns than those of men" because men usually cross the border independently whereas women rely primarily on female networks.[11] Once in the United States, many migrant parents, particularly women, discover that their lives become consumed with work. Gossip serves then as a cultural practice providing entertainment and enabling families to maintain connections across great geographical distances. Dreby says, "Gossip about the lives of family members in Mexico simultaneously connects them to those they have left behind and gives them a break, at least for a time, from the world of work that defines their lives abroad."[12]

Gossip is an essential way that women ensure their safety apart from border-crossings. When I was pregnant with both of my children, I spent a lot of time talking with other women. The experience of pregnancy and childbirth transcended the limits of language. Never before had I felt so connected to a larger web of life. At the same time, I had never before felt so out of control or overwhelmed by the utter mystery of my body as it was quickly stretched and transformed beyond what I perceived to be normal and comfortable proportions. During both of my pregnancies, I often found myself sitting around a table with women friends. Those who had already given birth shared their experiences. On many occasions, the experiences of other women who weren't present for the conversation were recounted in great detail. The point of our gossiping about them was to prepare ourselves as much as we could for the inevitable "what ifs" of pregnancy and the birthing room. Women can face a whole host of problems on their birth journey— high blood pressure, gestational diabetes, and breech presentation, to name a few. Giving birth can be risky even for women in our society who have access to health care insurance and reliable care. It is even riskier for those without access to reproductive care. God-sibs sitting with me around those tables helped me know that my feelings and worries mattered and that I was not alone.

Gossiping with other women became even more important when I experienced a miscarriage during my second pregnancy. To be honest, I was at first afraid to share the story of my miscarriage because I felt like a dismal failure. My hopes and dreams for a second child were lost in the rush of blood that my body expelled onto the bathroom floor. My head was filled with questions: What did I do wrong? Should I have chosen different foods? Should I have worked less? These feelings of failure were reinforced when people responded by saying "Everything happens for a reason." The hellfire and brimstone threat of God's judgment from my Southern Baptist upbringing reared its ugly head in the depths of my conscience as the thought passed through my mind that my miscarriage could be a punishment for past sins. As an ordained minister, theologian, and ethicist, I could dismiss some of these feelings as remnants of my earlier experience of conservative evangelical faith. Still, other questions and feelings lingered with me. What was most overwhelming was the feeling of being isolated and alone.

It was not until I started talking about this experience that I found out how common miscarriage was among women. Other women shared names of friends who had experienced miscarriage, not to highlight their misfortune, but to help me find a much-needed network of support. No other space or time in church or society was created to grieve the experience of loss publicly. Very few church communities ritualize the experience of miscarriage. Women are left to discover their own God-sibs. Gossiping with friends and hearing about others' experience of miscarriage became for me a way of ritualizing the experience. The friends who listened with sensitivity and compassion and shared the names of other women with a common experience became for me a visible sign of God's grace in the midst of loss.[13]

Thank God for God-sibs

Chloe is one of the first people outside of my family who I call or text when something is on my mind or something has happened that I need to review. We are both parents of young children with growing responsibilities for our aging parents. My mother, now in her eighties, has taken a couple of very hard falls. When I get a call from my brother to go to the emergency room, fear and adrenaline rush through my body with the force of an electric shock. I drop everything and head to the hospital.

A day or two after my last trip to the emergency room, I texted Chloe: "Gotta walk." She quickly responded: "5:45 AM tomorrow works for me." The early hour didn't matter this time because I wasn't sleeping at night anyway. When Chloe arrived at my door, I said to her with a feeling of desperation, "My parents have got to move out of that house. They need more help! Honestly, Chloe, I don't know if they can even afford to get more help." The truth was out, *sort of*.

A feeling of relief washed over my body as the real truth worked its way out of my psyche by sharing the nitty-gritty details of what had happened to my mother. I told Chloe all about how my mother couldn't remember how she fell. She developed a goose egg bump on her head that was the size of a baseball while we waited and waited and waited for a visit from the doctor in the hospital. My mother was in a great deal of pain the whole time we waited and the scenario made me feel helpless. It's hard to get used to shifting my role in my family of origin from being a dependent as a child, or the one being cared for, to acting as a caregiver for my aging parents. Ninety minutes of pounding the pavement gave me the time I needed to talk through the situation. When we arrived back at my house, Chloe quickly flipped through the pictures on her iPhone, turned the phone around so that I could see, and showed me a picture of her mother with a black eye. Her mother had just recently fallen at home as well. She said as she held up her phone, "I'm with you through this aging parent thing." Thank God and "God-sibs" that I am not alone.

Notes

1 See studies such as Joanna Dreby, "Gender and Transnational Gossip," *Qualitative Sociology* 32 (2009): 33–52; K. Van Vleet, "Partial Theories: On Gossip, Envy, and Ethnology," *Ethnography* 4 (2003): 491–519; S. Johnson, "A Game of Two Halves?: On Men, Football, and Gossip," *Journal of Gender Studies* 3 (1994): 145–54.

2 For more information on the origin of the term "gossip" and the rituals of baptism and churching in the Middle Ages, see Merry E. Wiesner-Hanks, "Women and Men, Together and Apart," in *Reformation Christianity,* edited by Peter Matheson (Minneapolis: Fortress Press, 2007), 152–53. I am indebted to her careful historical research here.

3 Maimonides drew this conclusion because of the Hebrew term used in Deut. 17:6 for witnesses, "*edim,*" is masculine in gender. See Shimshon Ettinger, "On the Place of Logic (Svara) in Mainmonides' Code," in *Authority, Process and Method: Studies in Jewish Law,* edited by Hanina Ben-Menahem and Neil S. Hecht (Amsterdam: Harwood Academic Publishers, 1998), 162.

4 Leopold Auerbach, *The Babylonian Talmud in Selection* (New York: Philosophical Library, 1944); accessed online at http://sacred-texts.com/jud/bata/bata00.htm.

5 Auerbach, *The Babylonian Talmud in Selection*, 20.

6 Ibid.

7 Lloyd Pietersen in "Women as Gossips and Busybodies? Another Look at 1 Timothy 5:13," *Lexington Theological Quarterly* 42.1 (2007): 21.

8 *Urban Dictionary* online. Accessed online at http://www.urbandictionary.com/define.php?term=gossip.

9 Matthew Feinberg, Robb Willer, Jennifer Stellar, and Dascher Keltner, "The Virtues of Gossip: Reputational Information Sharing as Prosocial Behavior," *The Journal of Psychology and Social Psychology* 102 (2012): 1015.

10 Joanna Dreby, "Gender and Transnational Gossip," 36.

11 Ibid.

12 Ibid.

13 See Monica A. Coleman on miscarriage in this volume for her reflections on the role that others, especially women, played in her healing (chapter 4).

Form your own circle for sacred sharing

Have you ever tried to create intentional space and time to cultivate transformative and healthy conversations with other women where you can share in the bonding aspects of gossip? Why not form a circle of sharing in which you and other women can share knowledge, pass along practical moral wisdom, and discern in community what you value most. You can begin by writing a covenant together that includes a regular time to meet, ensures that everyone in the circle has the space to contribute, includes confidentiality regarding the stories shared, and invites intentional listening. You might consider adopting a practice like passing a talking stick around the circle so that each person has time to speak and a clear way to enter the conversation. You and your sacred circle are free as women to define the rules.

Questions for discussion

1   Elizabeth argues that gossip "creates strong social bonds, serves as a way of sharing knowledge and enlarging social networks, enables women to discern in community what we value most, and provides a means of passing along practical moral wisdom." Think about your own experience of gossip. Are there gendered dimensions to your understanding of or experience of gossip (i.e., when you are with members of one sex or gender, do the topics you talk about or your level of vulnerability in sharing change?) How would you define constructive gossip, and its destructive forms?

2   This chapter seeks to (re)claim the definition of gossip that stereotypes of women obscure: the concept of gossip as "God-sib" as it originated in the Middle Ages, where "God-sibs" were to be "spiritual kin" and help the newborn children develop and grow in faith. Can and should "gossip" be retrieved in this way or do you think the word is hopelessly sullied with its negative connotations?

3   Elizabeth recounts a painful experience of miscarriage, where gossiping and girl-talk proved vital to her healing

process. Can you remember times in which women became "God-sibs" for you and gossip with friends became a sign of God's grace? If so, when and in what context?

4   While not the focus of this chapter, the author speaks positively about the role of ritual in women's lives: she argues that the practices of designating "God-sibs" and "churching" once served important functions and she laments the lack of rituals to mark miscarriage. What role does ritual play in the development of a healthy spiritual life? Are there other significant moments of a women's life that you think merit ritualization?

Suggestions for further reading

Chittister, Joan. *The Friendship of Women: The Hidden Tradition of the Bible*. New York: Bluebridge, 2006.

Holmes, Emily A. *Flesh Made Word: Medieval Women Mystics, Writing, and the Incarnation*. Waco, TX: Baylor University Press, 2013.

Moltmann-Wendel, Elisabeth. *Rediscovering Friendship: Awakening to the Power and Promise of Women's Friendships*. Minneapolis: Fortress Press, 2001.

8

Cursing God
(infertility)

Gina Messina

Growing up, I believed that motherhood was my destiny, an idea that was constantly reinforced by my family, church, teachers, and surrounding culture. I understood that women were supposed to become mothers, and as a female I aspired to such.

For as long as I can remember, my favorite form of play was caring for my baby dolls. It was training, really, preparing me for the only future I was certain I wanted to have. My mother often told me, "Just get through school, you don't need to be book smart; when you grow up you're going to get married and have kids." I dreamed of the day that this would happen; my destiny was to have the perfect husband, perfect marriage, and perfect children. No one ever told me that in real life there are no fairytale endings and there is no such thing as "perfect." Although I married a terrific man and have a great marriage, like any marriage, it is far from perfect. As for children, well, that didn't happen the way it was supposed to either.

I am Catholic; my husband, Chris, converted to Catholicism. We were married in the Catholic Church. We made a commitment to be a Catholic family, to raise our children Catholic, and honor the teachings of the Church. Ironically, it was those same teachings that played a critical role in my feelings of inadequacy and shame throughout my quest to become a mother.

During our Pre-Cana counseling session, our pastor reinforced the idea that as a woman—and a Catholic woman at that—having children was my priority. My pastor told me that once I was married, it would be my duty to leave my job and focus on becoming a mother. He said that I needed to "sacrifice" the life I had so that I could live out God's will and raise Catholic children. While I was young and still developing my feminist lens, his words did not sit well with me.

Regardless of the unsettled feelings I had about my pastor's demands, Chris and I had decided that children were very important to us. We wanted to leave the prospect of becoming parents in "God's hands." We committed to not using any form of birth control and believed that we would conceive when the time was right. It was three years into our marriage when we started to wonder why we had not yet been blessed with a child. We hadn't been particularly proactive other than behaving like newlyweds. I wasn't charting or taking my temperature. I wasn't using ovulation kits or researching methods to increase the likelihood of pregnancy. And so, I wasn't terribly worried then—I just thought that we needed some direction, so I reached out to my physician in hopes of receiving some.

I very clearly remember the feeling of sitting in my doctor's office surrounded by pictures of the birth canal and various stages of the birth process. I felt overwhelmed with joy—a little fearful of the birthing process itself—but joyful at the prospect of finally becoming a mother. I had no worries about my ability to have children and believed that one session of guidance with my doctor would open the door to motherhood.

My appointment went well and my doctor declared me to be in good health; she could see no reason why I should not be able to conceive. Chris was next to be evaluated and also was declared perfectly capable of producing offspring. So I started monitoring my temperature, charting, and noting the signs of ovulation. Another four years went by with no results. In between there were a lot of tears, a lot of sex, a lot of stress, and many arguments.

My mother's foretelling of my future and my pastor's words played over and over in my head. Although I had grown in those seven years and had a better grasp of the ways religion and culture oppress women, I still had a sinking feeling that I was failing as a woman, a wife, and a Catholic. I didn't know how to respond to my body's inabilities. I feared infertility treatments and was concerned about their ethical implications; the Catholic Church stands firmly against such medical interventions. Likewise, the prospect of adoption felt overwhelming.

Throughout college I had taken several women's studies classes and upon graduating, I had landed a job working in a domestic violence shelter. My feminist lens had gradually taken shape by being immersed in a world where women were escaping gender-based violence and questioning God's role in their abuse. I, too, began to engage in theodicy questions—I was not in an abusive marriage, but instead a questionable relationship with God—why wouldn't God allow me to fulfill my "duty" to my church and my family? Would God eventually reward me as Sarah was rewarded with Isaac? It was with these questions in mind that I pursued graduate school and began a journey that led me to realize that my cultural and religious beliefs conflicted with my evolved feminist identity. And while I was fully able to acknowledge rationally that no woman's worth is defined by her ability to give birth, I still embodied the expectations of my cultural and religious beliefs emotionally and psychologically. Although I could intellectually comprehend that my life served many purposes in this world, I perceived my value as diminished if I could not become a mother.

When my mom died, everything changed and my need to become a parent grew even stronger. Losing my mother suddenly was the most tragic and devastating moment I've experienced. With no warning, the one person who played the greatest role in my life was gone. Our relationship was suddenly over. While I would never again share in our mother-daughter bond, at least not in the physical sense, I thought I could mother my own child. After working through much grief, I moved past the many fears I had about fertility drugs and procedures and jumped in with both feet. However, after a year of failed treatments, nine years of infertility total, and a hopeless diagnosis from my infertility specialist, I felt shell-shocked.

I sank into a ritualistic cycle of grief that was all consuming. After 136 failed cycles, day 1 became a ritual day of grieving. I would sob uncontrollably, blame God for leaving me infertile, and appeal to my biblical foremothers who shared my barren state. Questioning whether God was punishing me for some bad act, or if perhaps infertility was simply my "cross to bear," I cried out with hopeless rage and cursed God for abandoning me, leaving me barren, and refusing me the one role that society and church demanded of me—a role I believed was my call. I reflected on the anguish Sarah must have felt in a time when women where solely valued for their childbearing abilities. While Sarah struggled with infertility, her husband Abraham had a child with Hagar, her Egyptian handmaid. Unable to conceive a child, Sarah felt worthless and was bitter that Hagar was able to give her husband an heir (Gen. 16). I shared in Rachel's envy of the many women around me realizing my dream of becoming a mother. As Rachel resented her sister who gave birth to seven children for the husband they shared (Gen. 29), I also have resented my "sisters" who have been blessed with the ability to give life. For six days I would lament my barren womb and once my blood flow ceased, I ended my mourning and turned to the hope of Hannah to continue my ritual. Hannah, whose womb was "closed" by the Lord (1 Sam. 1:5), prayed for a son with hope that she would not be forgotten (1 Sam. 1). I, too, pleaded with God to remember me and was filled with hope that my womb might be opened.

During my fourteen-day phase of "hope" I prayed to my foremothers and to Mary. There is no doubt that Catholic Marian doctrine played into my understanding of woman's role as mother. Teachings that Mary is the perfect woman because she is a mother and a virgin—an impossible feat for normal women to achieve— are oppressive and participated in my feelings of inadequacy. These patriarchal representations of Mary result in shame and leave women feeling they can never be as "good" as the Mother of Christ. However, I began to tear down those images in my mind and came to know Mary as a maternal friend; she has since become a major source of solace and strength.

Theological training certainly impacted my evolved understanding of Mary, but so did the women in my life. My grandmother had a statue of Mary in her home she knelt before daily. It was her place to worship and pray. Being orphaned at a young age, Mary was the mother she never had and thus it was Mary she always turned to, not God. Likewise, my mother also found strength in Mary. Because they were both women and both mothers, my mom felt that she could relate to Mary and thus, our home was decorated in her image.

Our Lady of Fatima played a particularly important role in our family. Mary appeared in this apparition to three children in Fatima in 1917 on the thirteenth day of the month for six consecutive months. During her last apparition, Mary performed "the Miracle of the Sun" as witnessed by seventy thousand people. Fatima was a story my mother grew up with and was evidence of Mary's relationship with her and the world. I came to know Our Lady of Fatima as our Mother who performed miracles—as the Mary to turn to when all seemed hopeless.

Although I live in Southern California where Our Lady of Guadalupe is central within the culture and there is little knowledge of Our Lady of Fatima, I fortuitously found a church that has a shrine of the Fatima Mother. It was St. Peter and Paul—the same name of the church where my mother graduated from the eighth grade, was married, baptized her first child, and was buried. Finding Our Lady of Fatima at St. Peter and Paul seemed like a divine mercy to me and I felt compelled to go to her. During my cyclical, two-week phase of hope, I would stand before Mary for hours praying, crying, pleading to be blessed with a child.

Although Mary has been imaged in ways that are oppressive and sexist, popular Marian devotion has resulted in a reimagining of Mary by women who have embraced her as a maternal friend. Mary shares in and affirms our everyday experiences as women such as sexuality and motherhood and is a key figure for understanding our lives. In Mary we certainly see a suffering mother; however, we also see a woman who is strong, supportive, nurturing, and relational. For me, Mary is a source of strength and as I looked for a modern-day miracle, Our Lady of Fatima offered me hope.

It was around day twenty that my desperation would take hold and complete the cycle. Although it was obvious that day one would surely arrive again, I would chart my symptoms, research them, and claim them to be possible signs of a pregnancy fearful that my grief-stricken state would resume soon.

As if this self-inflicted cycle of grief were not enough, it seemed that I was constantly surrounded by pregnant bellies. Every which way I turned, the women around me were expecting: sisters, cousins, friends, acquaintances—even random women at the grocery store. Although I wanted to be happy for them, Rachel's envy consumed me. I found myself having recurring dreams of throwing baby bottles at a pregnant friend's head—there's no need to deconstruct that! While embarrassed and ashamed by these feelings, I couldn't fight my jealously and anger. I felt alone and betrayed every time another woman close to me conceived.

I found comfort with a friend who also was struggling with infertility. We met weekly for lunch and shared our stories of pregnancy sightings, struggles with family, and anger over our inability to conceive. About a year passed when she shared her news that she was pregnant. In an attempt to be empathetic, she had emailed me the news to give me time to adjust before we spoke in person. I called her to congratulate her: I had wanted to be enthusiastic and share in her happiness, but instead found myself breaking down and sobbing on her voicemail. I said that I loved her, that I was so happy, and that I could not wait to hear all the details and meet her baby, but my wailing conveyed a different message. It was humiliating. Not only was I envious, but I was also losing my "infertility buddy." Not long after, we lost touch. It was too awkward for both of us.

Although I reached out for support to others, what I found was many who wanted to comment on my "non-condition" and share their own perspectives of what they thought was wrong with me. I often felt wounded by the many things those I counted as loved ones would express to me. While some statements were simply thoughtless, others were hurtful and representative of the societal mindset that women's value is tied primarily to their wombs.[2]

So many women would flippantly offer to carry a child for me; some women I knew well, some women I barely knew; but all thought it was such a simple thing and that they were offering me a reasonable solution to my infertility.

Some women told me that my problem was easily resolvable: if I would just stand on my head—seriously, stand on my head during intercourse—I would be sure to conceive. Others offered me advice on exactly what days and in what positions I should be having sex. And the most common statement I heard from both men and women was that I was just too stressed and needed to relax.

Here's some friendly advice: if you are speaking to a woman dealing with infertility, unless you want to put yourself at risk for serious injury, I would encourage you to refrain from saying any of these things.

Other comments were far more hurtful, though I don't believe the people sharing them realized they were inflicting wounds in their efforts to "help."

- I was told that I was lucky my husband hadn't left me yet for a woman who could give him a family. Most men, they said, would not tolerate such a failing by their wives.

- I was told that I should not speak of my infertility because it could be embarrassing for my husband; what if someone thought there was something wrong with *him*? His masculinity would surely be damaged if word got around.

- When considering artificial insemination and in-vitro fertilization some questioned why I did not want my child to be conceived out of love. In other words, didn't the use of modern science and technology somehow compromise any birth that would come as a result?

- Then of course, there were the many who objected to my eager attempts to get pregnant on theological-ethical grounds. What kind of person would I be if I were to keep challenging what God had apparently already decided was our fate?

Such statements about my failings as a woman and the embarrassment I was causing my husband are not uncommon for women struggling with infertility, though I only realized how damaging these notions were when they were directed at me. Clearly they draw on problematic theological interpretations that oppress women and deny our humanity while reinforcing the patriarchal order of church and society. Likewise, to claim that a child would be somehow "less than" if conceived with medical assistance denies the theological conviction that all humans are created in the image of God. And to argue that one should not attempt to achieve one's goal—whether it be pregnancy or otherwise—is to deny our roles as active agents in our own lives. Nonetheless, I was deeply wounded and struggled to look past these misogynistic and erroneous notions.

Graduate school served as a distraction from my infertility. But upon completing my doctoral degree, I was no longer able to keep myself preoccupied. My motherless state stared me in the face and I had to do something (more) about it. Chris and I began to consider adoption. Although we felt hopeful and saw a light at the end of the tunnel for the first time, we quickly found ourselves bombarded by more negative feedback from some of our loved ones. From the get go we were not-so-subtly told that an adopted child would never be "blood," and thus not be accepted into the family the way a birth child would. As if our decade-long struggle with infertility was not enough, several of our closest family members expressed a fear of their inability to look past the absence of their own genes in our future children if we grew our family through adoption.

Criticisms came from every direction. Why not spend the money on IVF and have a child of our own? A close friend told me that she was disappointed in me for taking the easy way out. If I would just hang in there and continue the treatments, surely I would conceive a child. Not only was our ten-year struggle being discounted, but our choice to move forward—our excitement that a child would bless our lives—was being crushed. The questions continued. What if we ended up with a kid that was a "lemon?" What if the child was not white—could we really handle raising a child of a different race than us? Would we be able to love a child that was not "*really* ours"? The heaviness in my heart was indescribable. Did I have to make a choice between acceptance from our family or our future child?

Regardless of all the negativity, Chris and I moved forward with our adoption plans. I returned to the shrine of Our Lady of Fatima and prayed for a miracle. We were shocked when, after just three weeks on the waiting list, we received the call that every adoptive family waits for. We were going to be parents to a nineteen-month little girl. Mary had answered my prayers. Our daughter Sarah came home just after Christmas and our lives were forever changed.

Once it was real and Sarah was home, our families came around and shared in our happiness to our great delight and relief. Relatives traveled from across the country to meet our newest addition. Chris and I were so proud, so overjoyed; finally, we had the family we had hoped for.

Although Chris and I were moving on, others in our circle seemed unable to do so. When we would introduce our daughter to them, a typical comment would be "Now that you adopted, you will get pregnant and have a baby of your own." I was always offended by such comments and would respond "Sarah *is* a baby of my own!" Again, people were well-intentioned, but gave no thought to what they were saying. I had finally become a mother, but for some reason, it was still not enough for them.

Although Sarah did not grow in my womb, she did grow in my heart and there is no doubt that she is my daughter and I am her mother—late-night feedings, kissing boo boos, changing diapers, nursing fevers, and giving all my love—this is what motherhood is about. And so, I work on remembering the good intentions of those around me and letting go of the anger and pain that comes with their careless remarks.

Sarah was only home with us for about three months when we were summoned to court. The judge ruled she had been placed with us in error. He granted custody to a biological relative and removed her from our home. The moment of the ruling is one I will never forget. I ran from the courtroom weeping and cried out, "What kind of God allows this to happen?"

It is impossible to articulate the anguish we endured. I was grief-stricken and inconsolable. I was enraged. God was not punishing me; I did nothing to deserve such cruelty. In that moment, I believed God was abusing me and so, like Job's wife, I cursed God. After losing Sarah, I gave up on motherhood. I did not want another child; she was not replaceable.

Again, I turned to Mary. I knew she shared my grief; Mary knew what it was to lose a child. I begged her to watch over Sarah, to ease my suffering.

Five months had passed when I was shocked to receive a call from our adoption worker. The relative who was granted custody of our daughter could no longer care for Sarah and asked that she be returned to us. Once again, Our Lady of Fatima performed a miracle. My daughter came home and our family was resurrected.

There is no doubt we have had a difficult journey, but our journey is not over. We are in love with our daughter, and we are grateful to Mary for resurrecting our family, but questions about infertility remain. Although we had psychologically closed the door on conceiving a child, health issues that arose for me several months after Sarah's return pushed that door open once again. Following an emergency blood transfusion and management of an ongoing struggle with anemia, I was told that in the best-case scenario, I should have an ablation (a burning of the uterine lining) and in the worst case I might need to have my uterus removed. Both meant ending any chance of ever becoming pregnant.

Despite having Sarah in our lives, despite being reconciled that we would not have biological children, the thought of purposefully ending any chance of conceiving a child threw me into a deep depression. Up until this point, I had continued to quietly engage in Hannah's hope. My ritualistic cycle of grief had not ceased, and I was not ready to let it go.

Several weeks after receiving the medical advice, I found myself having an intrusive exam in the office of an infertility specialist. Was I really going to put myself through all of this again? I cried through the exam. I cried through the doctor telling me that there was hope. And I cried all the way home as I thought about how I might betray my darling Sarah if I pursued the infertility treatment. Would she think she was not enough for us?

The truth of the matter is that I don't want to go through infertility treatments again, but I do want to have more children. I want Sarah to have siblings and I want to have a large family—I always have. I fear the adoption process after all we went through with Sarah. And although I love Sarah with all my being, I am resentful over missing so much time with her. I mourn the fact that I never heard her first words or saw her first steps, and I cannot help but wonder what it would be like to experience those moments as a mother.

The ongoing struggle of infertility has left me grappling with emotions I am still often unable to articulate. Feelings of inadequacy and lack of worth have been overwhelming at times as family members and friends have felt it necessary to not only acknowledge my struggle, but also offer commentary on what they think I should do. My grieving process has been ongoing and results from multiple factors including societal expectations of women's roles as mothers, personal feelings of failure, and lamenting the loss of a child that existed in my imagination.

At risk to my health, I have ignored medical advice because, as one friend told me, I have not "done my grief work." Yes, I have lamented my barren state, I have participated in my ongoing cycle of grief, but I have not yet found closure. Without having the recommended surgery or being menopausal I wonder if there is still a chance that I could conceive.

Chris and I continue to talk about more adoption. Recently, Sarah asked me if there was a baby in my tummy. She tells me she wants a sister. All of her friends' moms are pregnant and she wonders why her mom isn't too.

While I continue to struggle with infertility, in Sarah I have found salvation. Although I had cursed God when we lost her, it was in her loving embrace that I also reconciled my relationship with the divine. Who we are is created and shaped through relationships and it is through my relationship with Sarah that I have come to fully know myself and engage a fundamental relationship with God.

Redemption is not linked to suffering, but rather to grace and love. I have experienced such grace by becoming Sarah's mom.

My conception of motherhood influenced by my Catholic culture has also evolved. Typically, we associate motherhood with sacrifice, as did my pastor, and measure the commitment of a parent by what she is willing to forego in favor of her children. However, we must eliminate the tension between personhood and motherhood—surely this does not exist for fathers—and we must create space beyond stereotypes that are not confining for women. The relationship between mother and child should be characterized by love, not always sacrifice or duty.

I believe the imperfect stories of Sarah, Rachel, and Hannah reflect my own story and continue to give me hope. Each of these women struggled with infertility, anger, jealousy, bitterness, and an additional wide range of emotions. Yet, their continued efforts to challenge their own barren states, the judgment upon them by others because of it, and their eventual conceptions offer hope. While traditional interpretations of their stories attempt to construe these foremothers as passive; a feminist lens reveals that in these women we see active agents. Each offers an example of the ways that we can claim agency in our own lives and participate in creating the outcomes that we seek.

The figure of Mary in general and Our Lady of Fatima in particular has become a constant source of strength. As a mother, Mary has listened to my prayers; she has shared my grief and has responded with comfort and love. I am grateful for having been blessed with my darling Sarah—no doubt, she is a gift from Mary. As I continue on in this journey, I give thanks for my beautiful child, for the cherished moments only parenthood can bring, and for my family that will—one way or another—continue to grow. Because of these foremothers, I have hope against hope.

Note

1   On this point, see Kendra Hotz's reflections in this volume on voluntary childlessness (chapter 10). Kendra notes how difficult it is for others to believe she can be truly happy being married without children, which is why many people in her life attempt to construct substitute children for her through her students or her pet dog.

A prayer for righteous anger and grief

Mother Mary grant me grace
to acknowledge my anger without guilt
to grieve that for which I have sorrow
and to let go of cyclical stress so that I may find peace.

Grant me courage
to face daily challenges without fear
to accept that which I do not have control
and to turn prayer into action for that which I can change.

Grant me wisdom
to embrace moments of pure love
to welcome unexpected joys
and to recognize opportunities that come with hope.

Questions for discussion

1 Have you or anyone you know experienced infertility,
   adoption, or any of the other issues described here? How
   are/were your (or their) struggles similar to and different
   from the ones described here? Gina's struggles with infertility
   were shaped and intensified by cultural and religious beliefs
   that a woman's purpose is to become a mother. In what ways
   have these expectations made an impact on your life or the
   lives of your mother(s), sisters, aunts, or friends?

2 Offering support and comfort to people who are suffering is
   an important aspect of Christian community, but as we see
   in the chapter, well-intentioned but misguided support can
   sometimes cause deeper damage to the sufferer. How have you
   been supported and comforted in times of grief and struggle?
   How might we draw upon our own experiences of solace to
   help us do a better job of ministering to those in pain?

3 Experiences of loss, alienation, grief, and tragedy often
   raise questions about God's role in human suffering. What
   tragedies have you experienced in your life that have led you
   to question God's role in your suffering? What role has your

faith played in these questions and how have you responded to them?

4 Have you ever been angry with God in ways similar to what Gina describes? What do you think it means to "curse God"? What role has this anger played in your faith and your relationship to God? Even in the midst of her anger at God, Gina relied on Mary and other female figures in the Bible for hope, courage, and survival. What female faith figures are important to your spirituality? Are they biblical women? Historical figures? Women in your own life? How have these women helped to support you in your struggles?

Suggestions for further reading

Dollar, Ellen Painter. *No Easy Choice: A Story of Disability, Parenthood, and Faith in an Age of Advanced Reproduction.* Louisville, KY: Westminster John Knox Press, 2012.

Harwood, Karey. *The Infertility Treadmill: Feminist Ethics, Personal Choice, and the Use of Reproductive Technologies.* Chapel Hill: The University of North Carolina Press, 2007.

Weems, Renita J. *I Asked for Intimacy: Stories of Blessings, Betrayals, and Birthings.* San Diego, CA: Publishing/Editing Network, 1993.

9

Casting out fear
(death and dying)

Victoria Rue

On June 14, 2008, my mother, Catherine, died in our family home in Downey, California. She was eighty-four. My mother's life had declined for three years due to melanoma, strokes, and dementia. My father had been her constant caregiver. During the last several months, each of my seven sisters and brothers visited and offered help and comfort. We all gathered together in the last week of my mother's life. She could no longer eat or drink. Hospice counseled us that her current state, absent extraordinary intervention, would result in her dying within a week or two

She was not responsive on Saturday, the day of her death. The morning had started with the change of nurses from the night to day shifts. One of my brothers stood at the foot of the bed talking with the nurse about her pain medications. As I stood listening, watching my mother, I felt a surge of anger. All that medical talk was filling her room. I felt that was the wrong energy for this tender time. She needed deep peace and I was just as sure she needed scripture. I hurriedly left the room and returned with the book of Psalms and the Gospels. Sitting at her bedside, I leaned in close to her left ear and started to read Psalm 23.

> Oh God, you are my shepherd—
> I want nothing more.

You let me lie down in green meadows,
    You lead me beside restful waters:
    You refresh my soul . . .[1]

My mother suddenly turned her head toward me. Her eyes remained closed. I could feel her listening. My brother and the nurse stopped talking and moved out of the room. I continued to read and pray. It seemed her total focus became the scripture. I sensed that something in her was searching for how to get ready. She was looking for a pathway and this Psalm, so familiar to her, became her stepping stone. My sister Monica came in and sat on the other side of the bed. I continued to read passages from various Gospels and pieces of other Psalms. Her whole body seemed to relax, her breathing changed, and I could hear long spaces between her breaths. Suddenly she opened her eyes wide, looked up at something that was compelling, smiled gently, and closed her eyes half way. The nurse quickly called in my father and sisters and brothers. I continued to read, propelled now, feeling the sacred texts were somehow leading her, giving her a path and a promise as she met her death. There were longer spaces now between her breaths. The ancient words drove as a momentum toward the mystery of death. Sisters, brothers, and my father barely breathed. The text was the only sound. "My soul is thirsting for the living God." The prayers, a cadence, were delivering life to life's end. The last breath. "Is she gone?" someone asked. I kept reading. A brother raged with weeping and sisters cried out, holding one another. I kept reading on and on knowing that the hearing is the last to go in death.

An hour later, the nurse helped me wash my mother's body. This body had once been my home and was my pathway into this world. Filled with many emotions, especially deep gratitude, I gently wiped her face with warm water that had a delicate rose petal scent. I washed her hands and arms, her torso and legs, but the skin had no life to it. My mother was not there. It was so clear. But to honor her body was my honor.

Questions

My mother's dying challenged my own finitude and propelled me to go deeper into understanding the death process. I found myself asking these questions: What is death and should it be feared? What role does the body play in the dying process? Is gender a factor? Months later, these questions stayed with me when I was offered an opportunity to become a hospice spiritual care counselor. I was privileged to do this work for four years.

From my work in hospice, and in teaching religious studies, I believe what is needed is a new Christian approach to death and dying. Specifically, Christian body negativity has fueled women's fear of and disdain for their bodies. Certainly feminists have attempted to counter this by celebrating women's bodies in all shapes and colors. However, common approaches in Christian feminism have stopped short of valorizing women's bodies in the dying process.

We need a body-affirming theology, perhaps one based on the cycles of nature, the cycle of life and death, including the experience of our dissolving form. Traditionally, mind-body dualism and the theological concept of heaven drove Christians to emphasize the importance of the next life over this one. As a result of these beliefs, the body became an obstacle to one's spiritual journey toward heaven, something to be punished (as in practices of bodily mortification) or discarded. Thanks to the ideas of Augustine, the body was to be regarded as a bag of sinful impulses and temptations keeping us from God. But what of the core Christian message: the Incarnation?

Traditionally, Christianity limited the Incarnation to the body of Jesus. God took on flesh in the divinity/humanity of Jesus. But Christian feminist theologians suggest that we need to see Incarnation as belonging to each of us. Incarnation can be seen not as a static one-time event but a process in which living and dying is "Godding," to use Nelle Morton's word (n.b., God is not a noun but a verb) such that living and dying are connected as part of what God is. And further, Incarnation need not be confined to humanity. Sallie McFague offers the idea of the world being God's body: the cosmos as the body of God. Because of Incarnation, Christianity might have a special obligation to honor and embrace our bodies and our connectivity to all that is. Enfleshed in the breakdown of all bodies is a vulnerable God who is aching, suffering, in pain, and dependent. Imagine how the dying process for women might be affected if older women could feel that enfleshed in their withering bodies is a Divine Old Woman who is vulnerable and caring. The deterioration of a woman's body would not diminish that Divine

Old Woman, but re-imagine Her as the woman dies and releases her body, birthing the Divine Old Woman into the Mother of the Cosmos.

Fear

Christianity does not generally focus on death other than its relationship to the afterlife. Left unaddressed is the process of the body's shutting-down, the changes—gradual or immediate—that one experiences as aging and disease take over and the life-force slowly recedes. This silence breeds fear of death. The philosopher Susan Sontag feared death. Sontag struggled with breast cancer. She mistakenly felt that if she did not acknowledge the possibility of death, she could prevent its happening. Her fear was so fierce that she demanded her "community" to be her moral cheerleaders to push her to get better, to take another treatment for cancer, and never admit to, or speak about, dying. So it was that she would not talk with her son about her death and dying. Sontag's son David remembers how his mother was obsessed about death, fought it, and yet, was silent about it. She denied it any place in her psyche. Thus there was no process for her to examine her fear of death, no person to which she could whisper her fears, nothing to hold on to so death could turn itself inside out and reveal its process and place within the life cycle to her.

We struggle as humans to understand who we are in this universe. We reflect on the meaning of life and ask, "what is death?" The life/ death experience needs, begs for, our attention. This is not morbid. This is healthy. If we do not speak of it, if we live in fear of death, we will die in fear of death. To die fearfully is a terrible fate—and it could be so different. If a person can speak about her own life/ death, understanding for herself what her own life/dying/death process means, then perhaps she could die more easily.

While fear did not dominate my mother's dying process, for others, fear can control their experience of death. Fear can accentuate physical and psychic pain. Fear can close one off from relationships. Fear can stop the eyes from seeing, the ears from hearing, the nose from smelling, the mouth from speaking, the skin from feeling. Fear can wedge itself into one's body. Fear can take away one's sense of self.

How can one engage the dying process rather than fear it? Here is the story of "Helen," a woman I saw for a period of five months in hospice. Fear blocked her ability to come to terms with her dying process.

Helen

"You're the one I want to talk to. If there's an afterlife, am I going to burn?"

That's how our visits began. She'd been raised as a child on a steady diet of hellfire and damnation. In her adult life, such matters didn't seem important. She raised her children, worked with her husband's business, and took care of a mother who had not taken care of her. Her life was full. She had no time for hell.

She experienced heart failure as an older woman. She kept seeing a vision when she was taken to the hospital of a little man dressed as a genie, sitting cross-legged, with his back to her, who was looking at a shiny blackness. What did it mean? The vision filled her with fear.

Now in hospice, she sat and watched television everyday in her "comfort corner," a cushioned chair in the corner of her room. She watched preachers like an elderly couple who daily inveighed on hellfire and damnation. She became more and more afraid each day. Still, she watched that couple, hoping for answers.

At first I wondered if there was something in her life that she deeply regretted, something left broken. Perhaps that was why she was afraid of damnation. She scoured her memory, dredged up spankings of her children, moments where she'd been angry with her husband. No. That wasn't it.

I asked her if she had ever experienced a moment of peace. Suddenly she was full of memories. Once she had gone searching for answers to a local Catholic priest. But he didn't seem to take her questions seriously. Then she went to an elderly, Seventh Day Adventist couple. As they spoke with her, she felt from them a pervasive love and peace. Real Christians, she mused. Even as she recalled them, she felt that same deep love and peace.

A second memory: she was on a cruise with her husband. She was standing on the back of a boat at sunset. Suddenly she felt the oneness of everything. Time stopped. There was stillness. She was filled with peace. She wanted it to never end.

A third memory: she was driving on a back road outside of Phoenix. She pulled over. There was silence. Suddenly, she felt part of everything. There was no sense of time, she felt she could just sit there forever. She didn't want to drive into town—she just wanted to stay right there.

One more memory: she'd been on a balcony of a motel. She looked down and saw the road and saw how it curved and then turned. She recalled that she could not see what was around that corner. When she thought about that image, she wondered about it. Maybe that's me, she said, always wondering what's around that corner.

The question of whether she had ever experienced a moment of peace was the simple impetus for a deluge of crystal clear memories that rushed back to her. She had touched something vast and yet peaceful. As she recalled each memory, its gift of peace returned to her. But would the preaching television with its relentless threats of hell and damnation erase those memories?

Through many months of conversations with me, she told stories of being a sharecropper and surviving poverty with her children in tow. Their lives had gradually changed with her husband's good business sense. Somehow in each conversation, we would speak of that elderly Seventh Day Adventist couple, or the moment on the boat, or her driving outside of Phoenix, or the road where she couldn't see beyond its curve. Those were her touchstones: something she could carry in her pocket, recall for a moment, and feel her own sense of well-being. This is not to say that she never felt fear again. She went back and forth for months between well-being and fear. Sometimes it felt like her fears became so entangled within her that they were more like roots. It's hard work to uproot fears and expose them to the light so that they can gradually shrivel up.

As her death grew closer, Helen had a vision of being in heaven with her children and husband. She called it "my beautiful dream" and told her family about it. As she saw the joy in their faces, it became her prayer and another touchstone. Near the end, she began seeing a young girl peeking around corners. Perhaps this was her, calling herself home? Or perhaps it was a way to see around the corner to the road ahead.

At the end of each hospice visit, I would fill out a spiritual care clinical note. There's a category called "spiritual strengths" with subcategories to check off: sense of purpose in life, serenity/peace, reconciliation, belief in rituals, acceptance of prognosis, forgiveness, hope, and belief in life after death. At the beginning of my visits, I could not check any one of these categories. By the time of her death, I checked every one of them. Helen had faced her fears.

The body

Washing my mother's body allowed me to honor the memories I had of how my mother had honored her own body in her lifetime, including her ambivalence about aging. As I smoothed her hair on the pillow, I recalled how, at seventy, she stopped dyeing it and embraced her gray. As I washed her face, I remembered as a child watching her in the mirror carefully "putting on her face," as she called it, to cover her lines and wrinkles.

In my hospice work, particularly with women, I have seen how difficult it is for individuals to accept their finite, dissolving bodies. After all, throughout our lives as women, our bodies have represented an important part of who we think/feel we are. So perhaps it is no surprise that the body-struggles women encounter, particularly in aging, are met again in the dying process. It is confounding that in the dying experience, women must once again face the disturbing depth of female stereotypes that now reside, internalized, within ourselves: that women are powerless, always complaining, incapable, weak, helpless, wrinkled, ugly, smelly, indecisive, unintelligent, etc.

As the body begins to wither, one can feel trapped in a kind of cage. Freedom of movement is often curtailed; walking can be slow, or help is needed to move from one place to another or even in one's bed. It is often difficult for women to admit dependency and to receive care since we have been schooled to provide it to others. In the dying process, sensations, appetite, thinking processes, perceptions can be altered by pain or by pain management through medications. Many women, however, don't want to ask for help in managing pain, perhaps because we feel we can or must bear it. Whether in childbirth or menstruation, or just in dealing with "simpler" aches and pains, women learn from both religion and society to "bear the pain." When this message is internalized, women can continue to "grin and bear it" in their dying process, resulting in concealing the true extent of their pain and thus "not staying ahead of it" as per standard medical advice with medication.

Our bodies are the form in which we live in this world. In dying, the body itself experiences major changes. In my experience in hospice, women across ethnicities and class often tried to hide these changes. Body negation can be a reason that women curtail, limit, or don't allow family or other caregivers to offer assistance or relief through massage and soothing touch. Thus while there is need for assistance and comfort, women often recoil from touch or the visibility of their withering body. Sometimes this can take the form of not allowing friends or even family to see them, or insisting on their hospital bed being placed in an isolated room rather than in the midst of the family.

Religion can play a part in how people view their bodies and sexualities. The male body has been reified by Christianity, both literally and metaphorically, with images of God as Father and as Son. Christian liturgies often use masculine language for God such as "Father," "Lord," and a one-size-fits-all "He." In Catholicism, priestly leadership the church officially recognizes is exclusively male. Women's bodies, seen as other, are forced into the false dualism of "sinner" or "saint": they either represent earthiness/sexiness/the temptress and rebellious Eve/Lilith or the obedient/pure/chaste Virgin Mary. Christian body-negativism and sex-negativism have offered women two choices, the historical dualism of virgin/mother or fleshy whore. Imagine then how women, influenced by Christianity, can come to adulthood lacking in body care and positivity, and in the aging process continue those same trends. Thus by the time women enter the death and dying journey, those initial body-negative feelings have given way to greater depths of shame, where the women feel even more embarrassed and isolated.

Daniella

I sat for a year with a hospice patient named "Daniella." As she worked with and ultimately accepted her weakening woman's body, I sensed she was able to do this because she embraced a philosophy of life that included her body's death. She accepted her body's demise because she believed that her body in ashes continued to be part of this world by being recycled in the great wheel of the cosmos.

Each time I would see a hospice patient, I took notes to help me later create a written report of each visit. Daniella often said very memorable sentences and phrases. I wrote them down. In what follows, I've adapted and arranged some of those sentences and phrases into a "poetic journal" that charts her journey toward death.[2]

December 4, 2009: First visit
I'm operating on four burners today instead of six.
I've prepared for this.

January 13, 2010
I'm doing a thousand steps a day.
Getting up every thirty minutes to walk.
Got a timer to keep me on track.
When I can't get around
I'll stop eating and drinking
And force myself to die.
Dying is a person's last job.
I'm going to do it well.

January 28
I'm tired.
Wish I could just stop and it would be finished.
But other days I'm glad to be breathing
Glad to be with my family.

March 4
My arms feel like 600 pounds and my heart is racing.
I live with it.
But it's taking so long.
This is a pity party.
I've got goals for the next five months.
Not sure after that.
I can tell myself not to be negative, like my mother did.

March 12
Breathing difficult.
I edited my husband's work last night.
Felt so good to be useful.

March 18

Well it felt like I just couldn't get enough air
So I looked at the oxygen unit, wondered about it,
Discovered that the tubes were blocked partially as well as
　　leaking air!
Called the company. They changed machines.
Immediately had new energy and could breathe!
It just took figuring out what the problem was.

March 25

I'm sleeping later in the morning.

April 9

We don't get out of this alive, do we. . .

April 18

I'm going to miss me, because I like me.
I want my ashes to be part of the earth
Not in a plastic container that never feels the rain.

April 25

Short of breath, dark circles under my eyes.
I've had 74 trips around the sun
I'm on my 75th!

May 1

My genes connect me to the cosmos.
I hope I have unfinished business at the end.
That's what makes each day interesting . . .
Because it has unfinished business.

May 8

I learn something new everyday
That's my secret.
Yesterday, I learned how to make "touch books" for
　　my grandchildren.
Want to see them?

May 15

This is the new normal: red in the face, red eyes, deeper coughs,
   less energy.
I'm mispronouncing words, can't think of words, get confused.
I hear whistling
Like someone just pleasantly whistling.
At first I was afraid.
Then I asked myself,
Why am I assigning fear here?
So now I just witness it.

I'm a child of the universe.
My cells are part of all history.
And I want to be re-cycled.
When we lived in Jordan
I breathed the same cells that Jesus breathed.

May 23

I'm taking morphine once an hour.
And I've been thinking about meaning.
Religious symbols are empty for me.
The universe and becoming
And continuing through re-cycling
That's my meaning.

May 30

My sister, who I am the most like, will come for our last visit.
I'm taking lorazepam in addition to the morphine. It's helping.
I'm still vertical, but feel diminished.
I don't recognize myself. Woozy. Not me.
Different than the person you first met.

I think of my body as a library
That will soon cease to exist.

June 8

You know how you and I used to greet each other . . .
By touching elbows . . .
Because I was afraid of catching germs?
Well, I'm hugging everybody now.

I've seen the coroner's room
Through a key hole.
It felt peaceful.

June 16

Do you know how salmon spawn?
They lay their eggs after coming back
To the stream of their birth
And then they change color—pink, red—
And die.
They've been out at sea for four or five years
And return to their birthplace
To spawn and die.

June 23

My sister and I didn't say good-bye
We agreed to meet in the spring.
One of your hospice team said to me
"that's a long time . . ."
I felt sorry for that woman.
We are who we pretend to be
Even though we must be careful of what we pretend to be.

June 30

I don't have other things wrong with me, just my lungs.
So this is just taking a long time.
I'm too healthy.

July 6

It was all a rehearsal.
The fire trucks came, but they saw the "do not resuscitate" on
    the refrigerator.
Then they saw that the oxygen machine was off.
They turned it back on.
It was a good rehearsal.
Now we're ready.
Everybody had a chance to cry and express their fears.
I had a chance to feel what low oxygen saturation feels like.
Now everybody's on board.

July 13
That's it, I'm done.
I've decided to not eat or drink.
Dying will be just normal, ordinary.
The natural cycle of things.

Daniella wanted her hospital bed put in the center of the living room, facing a large window. There she could look out on a stately oak tree and hummingbird feeder with all of the comings and goings of those colorful, busy, mysterious creatures. In my last visit, I sat at Daniella's bedside, holding her hand. For a long time we were silent. Then, amid my tears, I thanked her for all our rich conversations and for what she had taught me about life and dying. I didn't try to hide how sad I was. She looked at me, smiled, and said "I loved. . . every one. . . of those visits."

Daniella died a day later. I do miss her, just like she said that she would miss herself. Her body, as a library of wisdom, would be gone, but some tiny speck of sand might still hold her.

Daniella's story offers us all a chance to witness how a person gradually comes to understand her transition toward death that includes the deterioration of her body.

Each day she witnessed her physical decline. She was on a journey. She was watching the signposts. She struggled and accepted their messages. Gradually, she let go and became part of the cosmos. With clarity of intention, her body-life ceased to live and was, to her way of believing, recycled. What is to be gained from her story is not whether she believed in an afterlife, but that she spent time getting to know, notice, and honor her deteriorating body. Daniella talked about her dying and accepted the role her body was playing in that process even to the point of knowing it was time for her body to stop eating and drinking.

In writing about these events, I realize that I was able to have with Daniella conversations about her death and dying—conversations I was not able to have with my own mother due to her dementia. With Daniella, we spoke of her decision to stop eating and drinking. My mother, in contrast, was no longer able to eat or swallow. With Daniella, I heard the clarity of her belief in recycling her body. My mother's faith about this life and the next was equally clear but in the end, we were not able to speak of it. I believe, however, that in my reading from the scriptures, we were communicating. Daniella prepared for her death consciously, with herself and her family. My mother's awareness of herself, her journey, and relationships faded slowly. But, in spite of her dementia, in her last twenty-four hours, she was able to summon clear words of love and insight for each of her eight children and our father. This was indeed a parting, conscious gift.

Reflection

I am seventy-one. I collect social security. Last week I filled out an application for a senior living residency that asked what year I might move there. I imagined myself at eighty, no longer teaching, in good health, and active. I imagined my spouse, Kathryn, who would at that time be turning seventy-one. I also imagined her being vital, in good health, and perhaps teaching part-time. My, time flies, I sigh, hearing the old cliché, but feeling it in my bones. Perhaps my mother's gift to me, along with my hospice experiences, is the lesson to not turn away from my own dying process, but to keep turning it over in my hand, like a piece of crystal that has many facets and many mysteries to behold.

Just as the sound of her daughter's voice reading scripture must have entered my mother's ear as an intimate reassurance, perhaps it was also a call to her inner self to open, release any fear and embrace the Spirit. In my Christian faith, death is a transition to the next life—a life after death with God. When it is accepted rather than feared, when death and dying are folded into our humanity and our culture, when the deteriorating body is experienced as part of the incarnational journey, then perhaps we can all live better and die better.

Note

1   This translation comes from Priests for Equality, *The Inclusive Bible: The First Egalitarian Translation*. Lanham, MD: Sheed and Ward, 2009.

2   I have received permission via email to use "Daniella's" words in this poetic journal format by her husband, Allen, on April 2, 2018 (n.b., his last name is omitted to protect his privacy).

In parting, I offer my imagined experience of Mary Magdalene at the tomb. Is it death? Is it life? May the mystery of Magdalene's space between her breaths come to you in your life/death and may you find your name called by the Spirit who is both within you and already embracing you.

A meditation on Mary Magdalene

This road is endless today. Every step is sorrow. I promised him I would not let his death stop his dream, that we would find a way to keep the community together, that we would go on loving and caring for one another and all we meet in the way he taught us. Such a look he had on his face . . . when he spoke about his death. . . . Such a strange beauty, like he'd thought a lot about it and knew something about it. I'm finally here . . . the cave. What?

No! Where are you?! Someone has stolen your body! Where . . . where are you? How can this be! There in the morning mist . . . someone is there . . . is someone? No . . . but I hear my name being called, Mary . . . Mary. The fullness of my name, the sound of it. . . . As if I'd never heard it before. As if this was the first time. The sound of me. Yes, you know the sound of me. I am hearing the sound of me. The fullness of me. My whole self. My body, life, all that I have done and thought . . . How can this . . . ? I came here in such sorrow such loss. Death took my Yeshua. But now something new is happening . . . opening in me. I put my arms around myself. I close my eyes. Each part of me . . . heart, blood, tissues, muscles . . . breathing deeply . . . slow and slower . . . no boundaries . . . part of . . . this garden, bushes, the air, the morning light warm on my skin . . . a pulsing . . . breathe . . . breathe . . . something being born . . . something dying, something moving on . . . the flower opens, slowly collapses, caught by earth to seed again . . . breathe . . . no breath . . . caught between breaths . . . space . . . no time . . . you are here now, aren't you Yeshua? This place between . . . you are between these breaths . . . I feel you here. Quietly . . . in me . . . in this garden . . . part of all that is . . . my name . . . your name . . . more myself than ever before.

Questions for discussion

1　The author's professional experience in hospice care has provided her with ample experiences of spiritual accompaniment with persons as they face their own mortality. What do you understand to be a "good death"? How might others (e.g., family members or professional caregivers) facilitate that for patients and loved ones?

2　Victoria offers a feminist reinterpretation of the doctrine of Incarnation, where it is not simply a "one-time event" that occurs in the person of Jesus, but something that happens to us all. What does it mean to think about "incarnation" in this way? And what are the implications?

3　Is Victoria arguing that death and the body's deterioration in dying is not something we should fear? Or that we should face our fears (as opposed to deny them) as we approach death and dying? What say you to this question?

4　The author implies that women, who have long been socialized into providing care for others, find it more difficult than men to receive care from others, with the result of their underreporting their pain. Do you know of examples of this either in your own life or in the lives of others?

Suggestions for further reading

Isherwood, Lisa, and Elizabeth Stuart. *Introducing Body Theology.* Sheffield: Sheffield Academic Press, 1998.

May, Melanie A. *A Body Knows: A Theopoetics of Death and Resurrection.* New York: Continuum, 1995.

Russell, Letty M., Kwok Pui-lan, Ada Maria Isasi-Diaz, and Katie Geneva Cannon, eds. *Inheriting Our Mothers' Gardens: Feminist Theology in Third World Perspective.* Louisville, KY: Westminster John Knox Press, 1988.

10

Happily ever after
(voluntary childlessness)

Kendra G. Hotz

For a Hoosier girl there is a clear path to a good life, a simple story that begins "once upon a time" and ends "happily ever after." And for many people, for most even, it is a good story, a good life. It really is. You meet a boy, fall in love, get married in your church, have children and bring them up right. You take casseroles to the potluck, play racehorse rummy or canasta with your friends, and coach your kids' baseball team. You watch them grow up and fall in love. You cry at their weddings and spoil their children. This is a good Hoosier life. There don't have to be any big adventures or drama; there is no need for a princess to be rescued by Prince Charming. (Those can be good stories too, but they aren't Hoosier stories.) Church, family, friends: these are the characters on the stage. If you have those right, then you can expect to live happily ever after.

I'm a Hoosier girl at heart. Born and reared in the German-heavy southwest corner of the state, I believe that the story of potlucks and card games, baseball and church is a good one. I believe in the story of church, family, and friends—and I don't have kids. Don't get me wrong, there are plenty of children in my life: nieces and nephews, children of friends, and the hoard of giggling goofballs you can find at church on any given Sunday. What I mean is that I haven't borne or adopted any children, and I don't want to. In fact,

I never did. Mine is a different kind of good story. It has its own "once upon a time," and I'm in the midst of my very own "happily ever after." I just went a little off script.

My story goes like this. Once upon a time there was a girl who played with her sisters on Saturday mornings. Usually we climbed trees and horsed around with the dogs. But if it were rainy or too cold, we would stay in and bring out our Raggedy Anne dolls. My sisters took on the role of "mom." This was an important job. Mom was responsible for cooking and organizing the women's auxiliary at the hospital. Mom got everyone ready for church and took care of anyone who was sick. My role was also important, but it was different: I was "Aunt Kendra." Aunt Kendra would swing you around by your arms, teach your Sunday School class, and keep your secrets. Aunt Kendra was an important part of Raggedy Anne's life, just like my own aunts were important to me.

When Aunt Kendra grew up, she met a boy and fell in love, had a wedding at her church, took casseroles to the potluck, played cards with her family, and went to baseball games and Tae Kwon Do classes with her nieces and nephews. There was no big drama, and no Prince Charming because this is a Hoosier story. This is a story of the deep, abiding love of a life partnership that simply makes sense; it's the story of family, friends, and church. It's a good story, but in a world that reveres babies and motherhood, many people imagine that a piece of my story is missing.

After the Raggedy Anne mornings and the wedding at church, shouldn't the plot turn to children? That's where my story goes off script. Being "Aunt Kendra" was always enough for me; it always made sense to me. Even as I matured, I was never drawn to motherhood, even though I love being an aunt to my sisters' children and to the children of my friends. There is no part of me deep inside that wishes I had kids of my own. I enjoy children and believe that how well we nurture, protect, educate, and provide for them is a central measure of our health as society, but I simply never found myself wanting to take on the role of a parent.

Despite a strong social norm that dictated what good Midwestern girls were supposed to want to be and do, even as a child that story felt too small to hold all of life's possibilities. I thought that maybe there are different kinds of happily ever after. Maybe not every girl meets a boy. Sometimes she meets another girl. Sometimes she lives by herself. Sometimes she wants to be a mother; sometimes she doesn't. All of these can be good stories. In fact, all of these can be *Christian* stories.[1]

Callings: The search for harmony

When my sisters and I played in the yard on early summer evenings, we would hear Mom calling to us from the back door to come in and wash up for supper. We felt the pull of the meal and were drawn by the sound of her calling to us. That childhood sense of being summoned and of feeling drawn is closely related to the idea of having a vocation, of being called or summoned to a task or to a way of life. We often use the word *vocation* to mean the wage-earning work we do, but the term also has a religious meaning. Its Latin root, *vocare*, is related to the idea of calling. Have you ever felt a strong impulse to volunteer for a charity or to form a relationship with a lonely homebound neighbor? That task is calling to you. It's a vocation, or at least it is part of your vocation. A vocation calls to us like a mother standing at the back door, and we feel drawn to it like a hungry child on a summer evening.

John Calvin was a Protestant reformer in the sixteenth century who offered some helpful metaphors for thinking about what our vocations are. He said that God grants every individual "a particular way of life" to serve as a "sentry post," complete with duties that must be heeded, so that we would not "heedlessly wander about throughout life." A vocation gives us a place to stand in the world and a sense of purpose. Every person has a calling and living into that calling brings a sense of coherence to life. If you fail to hear and respond to your calling, Calvin said, "There will be no harmony among the several parts of . . . life."[2]

When I consider my own calling to serve as a theologian and teacher, a clear relationship emerges between my own hungers and the work that summoned me; a strong sense of harmony also emerges between the tasks and relationships in my life. It's not a perfect harmony, of course. No life is, but the pieces feel like they fit. In theory, I might have been called to serve as a structural engineer or an artist, but I can confidently affirm that I was not. I know that because those topics never awoke my hunger (be glad of that next time you drive over a bridge that doesn't collapse or view a work of art that moves you!). No, it was the unanswerable questions about ultimate meaning we pursued in my college theology classes that summoned me. The ideas we considered in class and the questions they generated awoke a hunger I hadn't realized was present. I recall, early in my sophomore year, helping another student in my logic class and recognizing the moment when "the light came on" and he could see how to solve the problem we were working on. What delight! What a privilege to be present for and to facilitate that moment! To this day the whole mysterious tangle of questions that comprise theology draws me. And to this day, the delight in teaching, the satisfaction in witnessing the moment when learning happens has never abated. This is what a calling looks like.

What if we were to think about child-rearing as a vocation? What if, just as we are called into some relationships and tasks but not others, God summons some marriages to parenthood but not all? As Calvin put it, the tasks that summon us will come together into lives that "exhibit melody and harmony."[3] The idea that our vocation brings harmony to our lives suggests several important ideas for thinking about the role of children in our lives. First, the melody and harmony of our vocation anchors us. It keeps us from drifting through life aimlessly. The song gives us a sense of purpose and direction. We need a calling to give us a settled and measured judgment about our purpose as a Christian disciple. If parenting is a vocation, then it should provide those with children with a sense of purpose and direction. Second, the metaphor of harmony also assumes that every human identity is multifaceted. We cannot reduce a person to a single role that brings satisfaction. Just as different notes come together to produce a harmony, so different roles come together to form an identity. A woman cannot be reduced to "mother." That role may form one note in the song of a woman's life, but it must be in harmony with other notes if it is part of her vocation. Many women like myself find harmony without that note at all. We're all making music with our lives, but we're not all playing the same chords. Third, the song of our lives is joined to a great chorus of all the saints and of every creature as they wait for God's coming reign. Sometimes Calvin uses the metaphor of a sentry post for our vocations. Having a vocation feels like having a place where we belong, a place to stand and witness the work of God as it heals and restores our world. It is as though we take our place in an orchestra and turn our eyes to the conductor who draws the music each of us makes into a grand symphony. Because of this communal orientation of vocations, our identities are no longer simply our own. We are caught up in the broader purposes of God's coming reign. Our question then is not simply whether having or not having children will be gratifying for us personally, but also whether that choice is a faithful expression of what God is doing—through our lives—in the world. The choice for parenthood is bigger than what pleases me; it is also about God's reconciliation of all things.

Jesus displays this sense of vocation with respect to children in his own ministry. When the disciples tried to block children from coming to Jesus, seeing them as distractions and pests, Jesus chides them, saying "Let the little children come to me, and do not stop them." He welcomes children and assures his followers that they are included and welcomed in the reign of God. But Jesus does not take on the role of parenting himself. Instead "he laid his hands on them and went on his way" (Mt. 19:14-15). He went on his way, and "his way" led to places other than parenthood.

The idea that a vocation brings harmony to the parts of our lives helps us think about parenthood as a calling. Imagine a couple after the "once upon a time" of meeting, falling in love, and making vows to bind their lives together. They seek meaningful work, find a church home, and build a life together. When they envision their future, when they imagine what a good life looks like, do they see children?[4] Does their common life make more sense, do the pieces fit together, do the notes produce a harmony, if they become parents? Do they feel a strong, persistent urge to bear and rear children? Do they feel that something is missing if children are absent from their envisioned future? If they answer these questions "yes," then having children is calling to them. Being parents is, for this couple, a vocation. Rearing children will be part of "happily ever after" for them.

There are many reasons why a couple called to parenthood may not be able to answer the summons. Perhaps they are haunted by infertility, financially unable to care for a child, or are ineligible for adoption. None of these conditions negates the calling to parenthood, and the inability to fulfill that vocation is a tragedy that will produce very real pain. They may find other good and meaningful ways to live, but the tragedy of a missed calling will feel like a discordant note in the midst of beautiful song. The disharmony is not a punishment for moral wrongdoing; it is simply the sound that tragedy makes in our lives. Callings are powerful and missing one or being blocked from answering it is hard.

Now imagine this same couple after the "once upon a time" of meeting, falling in love, and binding their lives together. They seek ways to make meaningful contributions to their communities, find a church home, and build a life together. But when they envision their future the pieces don't fit together if children are present in their family. Their common life makes less sense and feels disharmonious when they picture themselves as parents. They feel no strong or persistent urge to rear children, and their lives feel full and whole without becoming parents. Instead, they find a sense of direction and purpose through other tasks and relationships. They find harmony and delight playing different kinds of chords. In this case, parenthood is not calling to them, and their "happily ever after" will be different from the first couple. The key for each individual and for each married couple is to find that place where they can stand in the world to watch for the reign of God, to find that task that summons them and wakes their hunger like a mother calling her children to dinner, to seek harmony among the parts of their lives.

But the very idea that a marriage without children can be a valid calling for a Christian is hard for many to accept. As a society, we have idealized visions of women as made for the nurturing and caregiving that is unique to motherhood and imagine that any woman who cannot fill that role must either feel incomplete or else be morally or emotionally flawed in some way. So deeply engrained is our sense that every woman must deeply yearn for children that many of my friends who have children have tried to construct some form of parenthood for me. They may imagine that my work as a teacher is an expression of my maternal instinct or that my dogs serve as substitute children. But I cannot serve my students as professor if I allow them to mistake my role for that of their mothers, and I miss the essential "dogness" of my dogs— the delight that is precisely *not* human—if I expect from them the emotional complexity of a child. The instinct for others who are parents to construct children for me is understandable. Many who are called to parenthood love their children so intensely that they cannot imagine anyone else not wanting that kind of relationship.

Parenthood brings harmony to the parts of their lives, and they cannot imagine someone else finding beauty in a different pattern. It is a failure of imagination, but an understandable one. Thinking of parenthood as a calling, though, may give us vocabulary for expanding our imaginations. What if life simply makes sense in my family without children in the way that it only makes sense for parents with children? Imagine a God creative enough to call to each individual and to each couple in ways that are particular, distinct, crafted just for them.

Rarely has anyone ever questioned my calling to be a theologian and a teacher. For the most part people trust that I know my own mind and heart in this matter. That opening others to the delights of learning calls to me, that questions about God and humanity tug at me persistently, these are not ordinarily subject to the scrutiny of others. But that I am not called to motherhood has regularly been questioned. "Oh, but you'll regret that," intoned one woman at a retreat I was leading. Another offered, when I was younger, that I would certainly change my mind when my "biological clock starts ticking." Not infrequently I have heard—usually from a speaker who did not know that I do not have children—that "it's such a *selfish* decision." Some Christian communities espouse the belief that bearing children is a married Christian woman's responsibility, that it is her path to salvation (1 Tim. 2:15). Others insist that God's command to "fill the earth" constitutes a cultural mandate for procreation (Gen. 1:28). These are questions with which anyone called to marriage but not parenthood must grapple. Does a marriage without children violate God's purposes for marriage? Is it selfish? I turn to these questions in the next section.

The child-hospitable marriage

On a lovely Saturday afternoon in August of 1996, I stood at the steps of the chancel of Rock Spring Presbyterian Church, holding the hands of my beloved, as our good friend and pastor read the "statement on the gift of marriage," which many people will recognize as the "dearly beloved" speech. The statement offers an interpretation of the meaning of marriage in light of Christian faith. These statements are remarkably similar across Christian denominations. Though their language may differ, Methodists, Roman Catholics, Presbyterians, Episcopalians, Baptists, and many others all seem to agree on the core ideas that "God gave us marriage for the well-being of human society, for the ordering of family life, and for the birth and nurture of children. God gave us marriage as a holy mystery in which a man and a woman are joined together and become one."[5]

Matt and I had talked at length about the wedding service. We were both graduate students in theology at the time and wanted to be sure to participate in every element of the service with integrity. It felt right to us to say, "Yes, this is why God gave us marriage," even though we had no intention of becoming parents ourselves. We had long ago discerned together that God was calling us to a common life and that our futures made no sense and felt like a jumbled, disharmonious mess without each other. But neither of us felt called to parenthood. So how could we say that God's intentions for marriage included "the birth and nurture of children"?

In its statement of the purpose of marriage, the liturgy summarizes a traditional understanding of the threefold purpose of marriage. The Latin terms for these three purposes are "*proles*," "*fides*," and "*sacramentum*." "*Proles*" means that God intended marriage as the institution in which children will be borne and reared. "*Fides*" means that God intended marriage as a remedy for sin, "for the well-being of human society." Marriage serves as the institution that channels and directs our sexual impulses, which sin has distorted, so they find healthy expression in relationships of mutuality and respect. "*Sacramentum*" names that "holy mystery" through which two lives are woven together and two persons come into deep and abiding physical and spiritual communion with one another.

Often Christians have assumed that affirming *proles* as a good of marriage means that every marriage should produce children unless there is some natural impediment to doing so. When prayer in the wedding service is offered, it often includes a petition for God to bless the marriage with children "if it is your will." Many assume that it *is* the will of God for marriages to be procreative unless the couple is infertile, past the age of childbearing, or perhaps in some special circumstance where child bearing would be a danger to the life or health of the mother.[6]

Certainly biblical authors regarded children as a blessing of marriage. Gen. 1:28 calls for humanity to "be fruitful and multiply, and fill the earth and subdue it." This command, however, was given to the human species, not to every individual and it presupposes a world with seemingly limitless resources compared to the demands a relatively small human population could make of it. As one author has pointed out, this is the first commandment in the Bible, and perhaps the only one that humanity—now at over seven billion people and occupying every continent on earth—has fulfilled. As a species, we can check this one off the list and perhaps try to make some progress on honoring our parents and loving our neighbors![7]

Biblical authors take as a favored theme the stories of barren women who were miraculously given a child—Sarah, Samson's mother, Hannah, and Elizabeth. Since birth control was virtually unheard of in the ancient world, there is a natural assumption that, unless infertile, sex between a man and a woman would always produce children. Marriage without children could only become a vocation—rather than a tragedy—with the advent of modern contraceptive methods. But this does not mean that such marriages are contrary to the will of God as expressed in the Bible. It means instead that we live in a new social context and need to think carefully about what possibilities that context opens for us and what obligations it imposes. The availability of safe and reliable contraception has opened a world of possibilities for women to enter the public sphere and shape our world in powerful ways. In an age of overpopulation and a planetary crisis prompted by industrialization and consumerism, the responsible use of contraceptives can take on the shape of a moral imperative. In a world already "filled and subdued" and with the technology to choose to become or not become parents, we suddenly have space to shape our relationships as parents and as marriage partners in new ways.

The New Testament shows us one way that a new social context can reshape our expectations about family. In a social context that largely assumed that the primary function of a woman was to produce an heir for her husband, the New Testament does not privilege childbearing or assume that we have a moral obligation to become parents. Jesus often scandalizes his listeners by upending traditional family values. When an admirer calls out "Blessed is the womb that bore you and the breasts that nursed you," Jesus refuses to allow the value his own mother to be reduced to her reproductive work, responding "Blessed rather are those who hear the word of God and obey it!" (Lk. 11:27-28). He redefined family, asking "who are my mother and my brothers" (Mk 3:33). Jesus called women into his community without asking them about their obligations as mothers or wives. In 1 Corinthians 7, in one of the lengthiest New Testament discussions of marriage, the Apostle Paul offers an extended reflection on the relationship between spouses. Some within the Corinthian church had argued for the superiority of celibacy, even insisting that married couples should abstain from sexual relations. Paul responds that husband and wife should freely give themselves to one another, even going so far as to insist that spouses do not have authority over their own bodies. He disrupted the traditional patriarchal assumption that men have authority of women's bodies and that the role of the woman is to submit by also arguing that wives have authority over their husbands' bodies and that submission is mutual. What is most striking, however, is that in this entire discussion of marriage, Paul never comments even once on procreation. He assumed that marriage was entered into for the sake of sating sexual desires: "It is better to marry than to be aflame with passion" (1 Cor. 7:9). In other words, Paul foregrounded *fides* as the primary good of marriage to such an extent that procreation was entirely dropped from his discussion.[8] For Paul, taking into consideration the new thing God was doing in Christ meant that all social relationships and obligations had to be reconsidered (Gal. 3:28). Marital relationships were no exception. None of this suggests that Jesus or the early church devalued children or parenthood. Rather, it suggests that the earliest Christian communities offered new alternatives to the traditional family structure. Children continued to be welcomed, parenthood continued to be valued, but the church also found ways to value new modes of life. We would do well to emulate this biblical model of responding to new circumstances with faithful changes.

So, what does this mean for a married couple that remains intentionally without children? How do our marriages honor the good of *proles*? First, it means that marriage, like the reign of God itself, is hospitable to children. Hospitality to children means that even the non-procreative marriage will be called to contribute to the protection, nurture, and education of future generations. Its partners will gladly support educational work in the church and public sphere. They will advocate for policies and practices that enhance recreational, healthcare, and cultural opportunities for children. The partners of a non-procreative marriage will serve as aunts and uncles, as teachers and advocates, and will gladly make sacrifices to promote the welfare of all children.

The second way that the non-procreative couple affirms *proles* as a good of marriage has to do with how they assess their place within the human community and the broader ecological context. Affirming *proles* means that marriage is the institution within which we take deliberate responsibility for continuing our species and for nurturing the next generation. As one ethicist put it, "We are stewards of the 'gene pool' of our species."[9] And more than the gene pool, we are stewards of existing children who stand in need of resources to survive and flourish. And we are stewards of an ecological order strained almost to the breaking point by our efforts to mine it for the resources we need to provide for those children. In a context of overpopulation and a planet that has perhaps reached its "carrying capacity,"[10] we must learn to affirm *proles* as a good of marriage in more sophisticated ways than simply assuming that every married couple is called to bear children. Being good stewards of the next generation and being good stewards of a distressed ecological system may mean that we ensure there are plenty of resources for the next generation by not adding to the strain on the planet with children of our own.

Christian marriages are called to be hospitable to children. Indeed, the entire Christian community is so called. We enact this in the baptismal vows we make to infants or in the promises offered at the dedication of a child. Affirming *proles* as a good of marriage might even indicate that Christians who are called to parenthood should ideally undertake that vocation within an exclusive, egalitarian, lifelong union.[11] But we can affirm that and also acknowledge that not every exclusive, egalitarian lifelong union will express its hospitality to children through parenthood.

It turns out that there are many paths to a good life for a Hoosier girl, many ways she might arrive at a happily ever after. She might be called to a lifelong partnership or to live a single life. She might be called to parenthood or to form a family without children. In each story she will seek harmony among the parts of her life; in each chapter she will look for ways to welcome children; and in every sentence she will cultivate the gift of self-giving. With harmony and hospitality she will craft her own happily ever after.

Notes

1 Becoming a parent is such a strong norm in our society that we have no ways to speak of life without children as part of one's immediate family that aren't awkward. The term *childless* usually implies infertility. The alternative, *childfree*, gives the impression that those without children view them as pests—like roaches!—to be free of. Even saying simply "without children" is problematic because very few of us live lives utterly isolated from children. Nevertheless, "without children" is the designation I have chosen as shorthand for those who choose not to rear children.

2 John Calvin, *Institutes of the Christian Religion*, translated by Ford Lewis Battles (Philadelphia: Westminster Press, 1960), 3.10.6.

3 John Calvin, *Golden Booklet of the True Christian Life*, translated by Henry J. Van Andel (Grand Rapids, MI: Baker Books, 1952), 11.

4 In this chapter I am only addressing the experience of being a married or partnered couple without children. Although these questions are also important for single people, the social pressure to become parents comes to bear on married couples differently than it does for single persons. I also do not restrict the term "married" to male-female couples, though again, the pressure to become parents will bear on them differently than it might on same-sex couples.

5 *Book of Common Worship* (Louisville, KY: Westminster John Knox Press, 1993), 113.

6 Pope Paul VI offered a theological rationale for the essentially procreative nature of marriage in his encyclical letter, *Humanae Vitae*. In this letter he argued that sex always expresses two inseparable meanings, one that is life-uniting and the other that is procreative. It is wrong, he argued, to introduce an artificial barrier, such as contraceptives, to separate the unitive meaning from the procreative. Likewise, it would also be wrong to pursue the procreative meaning, through artificial reproductive technologies such as in vitro fertilization, without the unitive act. A copy of the *Humanae Vitae* may be found at the Vatican's online archive: http://www.vatican.va/holy_father/paul_vi/encyclicals/documents/hf_p-vi_enc_25071968_humanae-vitae_en.html. In recent years, some evangelical communities associated with the Quiverfull Movement have also argued that the use of artificial contraceptives violates the will of God. More information can be found at www.quiverfull.com.

7 Bill McKibben, *Maybe One: A Case for Smaller Families* (New York: Penguin Books, 1998).

8 1 Tim. 1:15 does suggest motherhood is an obligation for a married woman. Though this letter is attributed to Paul, it likely originated decades after his death during a time when attitudes toward women's authority in the church had shifted significantly, perhaps partly as a result of an effort to deflect persecution by assimilating to Roman values, including a patriarchal view of the family. As historical contexts changed, Christians preached the Gospel in new ways. Historical contexts have shifted again since the late first century, and so we too will have to discern what the good news is for our own age.

9 James Gustafson, *Ethics from a Theocentric Perspective*, volume 2, *Ethics and Theology* (Chicago: University of Chicago Press, 1984), 165.

10 Sallie McFague, *Life Abundant: Rethinking Theology and Economy for a Planet in Peril* (Minneapolis: Fortress Press, 2000), 87–89.

11 This claim deserves its own careful exploration. Christian theology has traditionally affirmed that marriage is the normative context for child-rearing. But must it? Are other family arrangements equally well suited to Christian child-rearing? These questions fall beyond the scope of this chapter, but are important to take up.

Blessing

Blessed are you, O Creator God.
In the beginning you lingered in shadow and chaos;
You spoke, and evoked light and beauty,
Sighed, and sent forth vitality and harmony.
Linger over us as we seek our place in your world and work.
Goad us to be courageous in asking questions that unsettle our
    answers.
Make us attentive to the details that resist our systems and
    certainties.
Create in us curiosity and playfulness
As we nurture, sustain, and expand the living networks
of love, beauty, and justice that connect us to each other and to
    your world.
Grant us humility and determination
As we seek your light in the broken shards of creation
And commit ourselves to the repair of the world.
Blessed are you, O Ground of all we hold sacred,
Source of all that is whole and authentic,
Confluence of every connection that surrounds and sustains us,
For you have called us into work and relationships and granted
    us purpose.
For these and all good gifts we give you thanks.
Amen

Questions for discussion

1   Kendra talks about going "off script," which implies that
    there is a "right" way she's supposed to live. Do you ever
    feel this way? To what extent is this script you feel pressured
    to follow shaped by expectations about how Christian
    women are supposed to live? By cultural or regional
    expectations concerning proper behavior?

2   Do you know couples who have chosen not to have
    children? How have you, and to your knowledge others,
    responded to their decision? Some people criticize couples
    who choose not to have children as selfish. Others say that

the desire to have children is selfish. What does it mean to be selfish or selfless in relation to children?

3 Drawing upon Calvin, Kendra describes "calling" or vocation as something that brings harmony to the rest of our lives. How would you tell the story of your own vocation? What are the things in your life that you feel called to do and be? Is your sense of "calling" religious?

4 What do you think about the idea of parenting as a vocation? How might Kendra's approach to childbearing change how people approach marriage and families or what some feminists have criticized as the pressures of "compulsory motherhood"? Do you think most women with children became mothers because they genuinely wanted kids or because they thought they were supposed to have them?

Suggestions for further reading

Cahill, Lisa Sowle. *Family: A Christian Social Perspective*. Minneapolis: Fortress Press, 2000.

Isherwood, Lisa, ed. *The Good News of the Body: Sexual Theology and Feminism*. New York: New York University Press, 2001.

Schottroff, Luise. *Lydia's Impatient Sisters: A Feminist Social History of Early Christianity*. Louisville, KY: Westminster John Knox Press, 1995.

LIST OF
CONTRIBUTORS

Monica A. Coleman is Professor of Africana Studies at University of Delaware. An ordained minister in the African Methodist Episcopal (A.M.E) Church, Coleman works in the fields of process and liberation theologies, African American religions, and theologies for social justice. Coleman is the author or editor of six books, including *Bipolar Faith: A Black Woman's Journey with Depression and Faith* (Fortress, 2016) and *Making a Way Out of No Way: A Womanist Theology* (Fortress, 2008). She has held various leadership positions in the American Academy of Religion, where she is currently on the standing committee for Persons with Disability in the Profession. Coleman speaks widely on religion and sexuality, religious pluralism, mental health, and sexual and domestic violence. Learn more about her at MonicaAColeman.com

María Teresa (MT) Dávila is an unaffiliated scholar and formerly Associate Professor of Christian Ethics at Andover Newton Theological School. Her activist focus and publications include works on race, racial justice, and theological ethics; Latino/a and *mujerista* ethics and public theology; Latino/a ethics and the ethics of the use of force; immigration; and the use of the social sciences in Christian ethics. Along with Agnes Brazal, she is the coeditor of *Living With(out) Borders: Theological Ethics and Peoples on the Move* (Orbis, 2016). Her main scholarly and activist concern is the question of Christian discipleship in the US context. On this front, Dávila integrates her scholarly production with homeless ministries, community organizing, and local advocacy efforts around issues of family homelessness, refugee welcome and care, and racial justice. She is a Roman Catholic laywoman.

Elizabeth Hinson-Hasty is Professor of Theology, Chair of the Department of Theology, and Director of the Peace Studies program at Bellarmine University. Her research interests include economic ethics, social gospel theology, feminist theology, and recovering the work of neglected women theologians. *The Problem of Wealth: A Christian Response to a Culture of Affluence* (Orbis, 2017) is her most recent book. She will be undertaking a new book project in 2019 entitled *Seeking More than Dutiful Love: God's Healing in the Context of Families Affected by Mental Illness.* She is Minister of Word and Sacrament in the Presbyterian Church (U.S.A.) and has served on several advocacy committees for her denomination. Among other awards and academic honors, she is a recipient of the Louisville Institute's Sabbatical Grant for Researchers, a Fulbright Scholar, and a Wilson Wyatt Fellow.

Kendra G. Hotz is the Robert R. Waller Chair of Population Health and Associate Professor of Religious Studies at Rhodes College. Her teaching and research interests focus on health equity, with special attention to racial and ethnic minorities. Her publications focus on the relationship between religious belonging and health-seeking behaviors and on the theological commitments implicit in the practices of healthcare providers. She is the coauthor of four books, including *Dust and Breath: Faith, Health, and Why the Church Should Care about Both* (Eerdmans, 2012) and *Transforming Care: A Christian Vision of Nursing Practice* (Eerdmans, 2005). She serves as Faculty-in-Residence and Academic Chair of the Ethics Committee at Le Bonheur Children's Hospital. She is ordained in the Presbyterian Church (U.S.A.).

Grace Yia-Hei Kao is Professor of Ethics at Claremont School of Theology and codirector of their Center for Sexuality, Gender, and Religion. Her teaching and research interests include rights (human and animal), religion in the public sphere in the United States, ecofeminism, and Asian American Christianity. She is the author of *Grounding Human Rights in a Pluralist World* (Georgetown University Press, 2011) and coeditor of *Asian American Christian Ethics* (Baylor University Press, 2015)—the first book of its kind. As a Presbyterian Church (U.S.A.) laywoman, she blogs regularly at "Feminism and Religion," holds leadership positions in several professional organizations (the American Academy of Religion, the Society for Christian Ethics, the Pacific, Asian, and North American Asian Women in Theology and Ministry), and is writing a book on the feminist ethics of surrogacy. Learn more about her at drgracekao.com.

Grace Ji-Sun Kim is Associate Professor of Theology at Earlham School of Religion. She is the author or editor of fifteen books—recent titles include *Mother Daughter Speak* (FAR Press, 2017); *Intercultural Ministry* (Judson, 2017); *Planetary Solidarity* (Fortress, 2017); *Embracing the Other* (Eerdmans, 2015); *Here I Am* (Judson, 2015); *Contemplations from the Heart* (Wipf & Stock, 2014); and *The Grace of Sophia* (Wipf & Stock, 2010).

She is a coeditor for the Palgrave Macmillan Book Series, "Asian Christianity in Diaspora." Kim is an ordained Presbyterian Church (U.S.A.) minister and blogs regularly on *The Huffington Post* and *Feminist Studies in Religion*. She has also written for *TIME*, *The Nation*, and *The Feminist Wire*. Learn more about her at gracejisunkim.wordpress.com.

Gina Messina is a feminist scholar, Catholic theologian, and activist. She serves as Associate Professor of Religious Studies at Ursuline College and is cofounder of FeminismandReligion.com. Messina writes for *The Huffington Post*, and is author or editor of five books including *Women Religion Revolution* (Feminist Studies in Religion Books, 2017) and *Jesus in the White House* (FAR Press, 2017). Messina is a widely sought-after speaker and has presented across the United States at universities, organizations, conferences, and on national platforms including appearances on MSNBC, Tavis Smiley, NPR, and the TEDx stage. She has also spoken at the Commission on the Status of Women at the United Nations to discuss matters impacting the lives of women around the world. Messina is active in movements to end violence against women and explores opportunities for spiritual healing. Learn more about her at ginamessina.com; connect with her on Twitter @GMessinaPhD and Facebook.

Marcia Mount Shoop is an author, theologian, and pastor. Ordained in the Presbyterian Church (U.S.A.), she currently serves as Pastor/Head of Staff at Grace Covenant Presbyterian Church in Asheville, NC. She leads and facilitates in churches, in the academy, and in community contexts around issues of race, gender, sexual violence, abusive power, and more. Marcia is the author of *Let the Bones Dance: Embodiment and the Body of Christ* (Westminster John Knox, 2010) and *Touchdowns for Jesus: Lifting the Veil on Big-Time Sports* (Cascade, 2014). She coauthored *A Body Broken, A Body Betrayed: Race, Memory, and Eucharist in White Dominant Churches* (Cascade, 2015) with Mary McClintock-Fulkerson. Learn more about her at marciamountshoop.com.

Kate Ott is a feminist, catholic scholar addressing everyday ethics issues. She lectures and leads workshops across the country on sexuality and technology issues related to children, teens, young adults, and parents. She is Associate Professor of Christian Social Ethics at Drew University Theological School in Madison, NJ. She is author of *Sex + Faith: Talking with Your Child from Birth to Adolescence* (Westminster John Knox, 2013), coeditor of *Faith, Feminism, and Scholarship: The Next Generation* (Palgrave MacMillan, 2011), and author of the forthcoming *Christian Ethics in a Digital Society* (Rowman & Littlefield). Learn more about her at kateott.org.

Ellen Ott Marshall is Associate Professor of Christian Ethics and Conflict Transformation at Candler School of Theology, Emory University. Her work in Christian ethics focuses on violence, peacebuilding, conflict transformation, gender and moral agency, and the dynamic relationship between faith, history, and ethics. She has edited two volumes of essays on peacebuilding and conflict transformation, respectively, and authored three books: *Though the Fig Tree Does Not Blossom: Toward a Responsible Theology of Christian Hope* (Abingdon, 2006), *Christians in the Public Square* (Abingdon, 2008), and *An Introduction to Christian Ethics* (Westminster John Knox, 2018). A lifelong Methodist, Marshall has also worked with the refugee resettlement program of the United Methodist Committee on Relief (UMCOR) and served as the lead writer for *God's Renewed Creation*, a pastoral letter from the Council of Bishops of the United Methodist Church.

Rebecca Todd Peters is Professor of Religious Studies and Director of the Poverty and Social Justice Program at Elon University. Her work as a feminist social ethicist is focused on globalization, economic, environmental, and reproductive justice. Her book, In *Search of the Good Life: The Ethics of Globalization* (Continuum, 2004), won the 2003 Trinity Book Prize and her most recent book is *Trust Women: A Progressive Christian Argument for Reproductive Justice* (Beacon, 2018). Ordained in the Presbyterian Church (U.S.A.), she has been active denominationally and ecumenically for more than twenty-five years and currently represents the PC(USA) as a member of the Faith and Order Standing Commission of the World Council of Churches and is a Public Fellow at the Public Religion Research Institute (PRRI). Learn more about her at rebeccatoddpeters.com and read her blog at patheos.com/blogs/todojustice/.

Victoria Rue is a university lecturer, a theater writer/director, and a Roman Catholic woman priest. From 2008 to 2012, Rue served as a Hospice Spiritual Care Counselor for VNA Hospice in Salinas, California. Rue lectures in Comparative Religious Studies, Women's Studies and Creative Arts at San Jose State University. Her book *Acting Religious: Theatre as Pedagogy in Religious Studies* (Wipf & Stock, 2010) introduces teachers and students to embodied/enacted learning. Her theater work is currently focused on interpreting and enacting scriptures from the world's religions as part of InterFaith Theatre. Her most recent plays are *Mary/Maryam in Christian and Islamic Traditions* (2017), and *Women of the Exodus: Faithful Resistance in Jewish and Islamic Traditions* (2018). Rue was a Fulbright Scholar at Dar Al Kalima University in Bethlehem, Palestine, Occupied Territories in Fall 2018. Learn more about her at victoriarue.com.

INDEX

struggle   4, 7, 10, 11, 19, 23, 42,
49, 53, 84, 112, 123–4,
125, 128, 129, 136,
139, 145
substitutionary theories   99 n.4
suffering   10, 37, 47, 95, 96,
98, 99 n.3, 123, 127,
129, 135
support   2, 11, 18, 20, 21, 25, 27,
28 n.1, 33, 84, 86, 107,
109, 112, 114, 124, 158
survival strategies   77–8

T., Mary   94
Talmud   109
Ten Commandments   46
theodicy   121
theology   3, 4, 5, 10, 12, 18,
46, 48, 73, 78, 95, 110,
122, 125, 135, 152,
156, 161 n.11. *See
also* feminist theology;
liberation theology
Thompson, Tracy   65
Torah   46
Tractate Kiddushin   109
trauma   90, 91, 94, 95, 99 n.3
Trump, Donald   1, 2
trust   24, 68, 97, 155
truth   22, 35, 40, 67, 92, 93, 94,
97, 98, 112, 115, 128
Turton, Anna   ix

United Auto Workers (UAW)   64
United States   1, 2, 46, 77,
80, 81, 82, 106,
111, 113

values   ix, 4, 10, 19–22, 25, 35,
46, 49, 53, 57, 63, 71,
81, 108, 111–12, 121–2,
124, 157, 158
Vianes, Jessica   28 n.1

virginity   19, 23, 24, 122, 140
vocations   10, 151–2, 153, 157
vows   19, 21, 57, 83, 95, 97,
100, 110, 123, 134, 147,
153, 159

Wales, Elizabeth   ix
Walker, Alice   5
Welsh Missionaries   100
Wesley Study Bible   36
West, Traci C.   12 n.8
Western Christian
thought   110
Western theological
tradition   99 n.6
Whitehead, Alfred North   66
white supremacy   6, 80
widows   51, 110
Williams, Delores   5, 99 n.5
wisdom   3, 10, 11, 24, 28 n.1,
94, 97, 145. *See also*
moral wisdom
womanism/womanist   5, 9
women   26, 70, 82, 152,
154, 155
Asian American   83, 84
barren   68–70, 121–2,
128–9, 157
bodies   135, 140, 158
church   106
in church leadership   85 n.4,
161 n.8
conversations   106, 108
devaluation   21
experience   107
as gossipers   106
idleness of   110
at Jesus's empty tomb   27
lives in Bible   18
love   18, 21, 23, 52
in Middle Ages   107
power   24
relationships   18, 28

www.ingramcontent.com/pod-product-compliance
Ingram Content Group UK Ltd.
Pitfield, Milton Keynes, MK11 3LW, UK
UKHW020735280225
455688UK00012B/670